SPEAK KOREAN WITH CONFIDENCE

ESSENTIAL KOREAN

PHRASEBOOK & DICTIONARY

Soyeung Koh & Gene Baik

TUTTLE Publishing

Tokyo | Rutland, Vermont | Singapore

Contents

The Basics

Introduction		4
Pronunciation guide		5
Basic grammar		8

1. The Basics   **12-27**

1.1	Personal details	13
1.2	Today or tomorrow?	14
1.3	What time is it?	16
1.4	One, two, three...	18
1.5	The weather	21
1.6	Here, there...	23
1.7	What does that sign say?	24
1.8	Legal holidays	26

2. Meet and Greet   **28-35**

2.1	Greetings	29
2.2	Asking a question	30
2.3	How to reply	32
2.4	Thank you	33
2.5	I'm sorry	34
2.6	What do you think?	34

3. Small Talk   **36-49**

3.1	Introductions	37
3.2	I beg your pardon?	40
3.3	Starting/ending a conversation	42
3.4	A chat about the weather	42
3.5	Hobbies	43
3.6	Invitations	44
3.7	Paying a compliment	45
3.8	Intimate comments/ questions	46
3.9	Congratulations and condolences	47
3.10	Arrangements	47
3.11	Being the host(ess)	48
3.12	Saying good-bye	49

4. Eating Out   **50-59**

4.1	At the restaurant	51
4.2	Ordering	52
4.3	The bill	56
4.4	Complaints	56
4.5	Paying a compliment	57
4.6	The menu	58
4.7	Alphabetical list of dishes	58

5. Getting Around   **60-71**

5.1	Asking directions	61
5.2	Traffic signs	63
5.3	The car	64
5.4	Renting a car	65
5.5	Breakdowns and repairs	66
5.6	Motorcycles and bicycles	68
5.7	The gas station	70
5.8	Hitchhiking	71

6. Arrival and Departure   **72-83**

6.1	General	73
6.2	Customs	75
6.3	Luggage	76

6.4 Questions to
    passengers   77
6.5 Tickets   78
6.6 Information   80
6.7 Airplanes   82
6.8 Trains   82
6.9 Taxis   82

7. A Place to Stay   84-93
7.1 General   85
7.2 Hotels/B&Bs/
    apartments/
    holiday rentals   86
7.3 Complaints   88
7.4 Departure   89
7.5 Camping/backpacking 90

8. Money Matters   94-97
8.1 Banks   95
8.2 Settling the bill   96

9. Mail, Phone and Internet 98-105
9.1 Mail   99
9.2 Telephone   101
9.3 Internet   105

10. Shopping   106-117
10.1 Shopping
     conversations   108
10.2 Food   110
10.3 Clothing and shoes 111
10.4 Photographs and
     electronic goods 113
10.5 At the hairdresser 115

11. Tourist Activities   118-125
11.1 Places of interest 119
11.2 Going out   122
11.3 Booking tickets   124

12. Sports Activities   126-129
12.1 Sporting questions 127
12.2 By the waterfront 128
12.3 In the snow   129

13. Health Matters   130-139
13.1 Calling a doctor   131
13.2 What's wrong?   132
13.3 The consultation   133
13.4 Medications and
     prescriptions   136
13.5 At the dentist   137

14. Emergencies   140-147
14.1 Asking for help   141
14.2 Lost items   142
14.3 Accidents   143
14.4 Theft   144
14.5 Missing person   144
14.6 The police   146

15. English-Korean Dictionary 148-191

The Basics

Introduction

• •

Welcome to the Tuttle Essential Language series, covering all of the most popular Asian languages. These books are basic guides to communicating in the language. They're concise, accessible and easy to understand, and you'll find them indispensable on your trip abroad to get you where you want to go, pay the right prices and do everything you're planning to do.

This guide is divided into 14 themed sections and starts with a pronunciation table which explains the phonetic pronunciation of all the words and sentences you'll need to know, and a basic grammar guide which will help you construct basic sentences in the language. At the end of the book is an extensive English–Korean dictionary.

Throughout the book you'll come across boxes with a 🖐 symbol beside them. These are designed to help you if you can't understand what your listener is saying to you. Hand the book over to them and encourage them to point to the appropriate answer to the question you are asking.

Other boxes in the book—this time without the 🖐 symbol—give alphabetical listings of themed words with their English translations beside them.

For extra clarity, we have put all phonetic pronunciations of the foreign language terms in italics.

This book covers all topics you are likely to come across during the course of a visit, from reserving a room for the night to ordering food and drinks at a restaurant and what to do if you lose your credit cards and money. With over 2,000 commonly used words and essential sentences at your fingertips you can rest assured that you will be able to get by in all situations, so let **Essential Korean** become your passport to learning to speak with confidence!

Pronunciation guide

Transcriptions

Korean words and expressions in this book are romanized using the Revised Romanization of Korean prepared and authorized by the Korean Government. Along with the principles of this system, some transcription conventions are adopted as follows:

(a) Words are romanized according to sound rather than to Korean spelling. However, in the case of verbs in the dictionary, the transcription of tensed sounds has been minimized so that the user can identify and utilize the verb stem without much confusion (e.g. to be = *itda*, instead of *itta*).

(b) Where there is an expression consisting of more than one word, a space is given to mark the word boundary.

(c) Three dots (...) are used in a grammatical phrase where a noun is required.

(e) In the dictionary, a hyphen (-) is used to indicate a verb stem or the optional adjective form derived from an adjectival verb.

(f) In the dictionary, for descriptive words, both adjectival verb forms (e.g., to be pretty = *yeppeuda*) and adjective forms (e.g., pretty = *yeppeun*) are given.

The Korean alphabet and its romanization

1) Consonants

(a) Simple consonants

ㄱ	*g, k*	ㄴ	*n*	ㄷ	*d, t*	ㄹ	*r, l*	ㅁ	*m*
ㅂ	*b, p*	ㅅ	*s*	ㅇ	*ng*	ㅈ	*j*	ㅊ	*ch*
ㅋ	*k*	ㅌ	*t*	ㅍ	*p*	ㅎ	*h*		

(b) Double consonants

| ㄲ *kk* | ㄸ *tt* | ㅃ *pp* | ㅆ *ss* | ㅉ *jj* |

2) Vowels

(a) Simple vowels

| ㅏ *a* | ㅓ *eo* | ㅗ *o* | ㅜ *u* | ㅡ *eu* |
| ㅣ *i* | ㅐ *ae* | ㅔ *e* | ㅚ *oe* | ㅟ *wi* |

(b) Compound vowels

ㅑ *ya*	ㅕ *yeo*	ㅛ *yo*	ㅠ *yu*	ㅒ *yae*
ㅖ *ye*	ㅘ *wa*	ㅙ *wae*	ㅝ *wo*	ㅞ *we*
ㅢ *ui*				

Reading romanized Korean

There is a very important distinction between the reading of romanized Korean and English. The Korean romanization system depicts the sound of Korean in English letters to help foreigners communicate in Korean. Because English letters used in romanized Korean are sound symbols, they have to be pronounced in a certain way only. They should not be treated as those in English words. In English words, the sound value assigned to a certain letter varies according to different words. For example, 'a' in *apple, father, syllable* and *date* all have different sound values. Unless you have learnt the English phonetic symbols, you might read the romanized Korean *a* differently from the expected sound depending on what romanized Korean words you have. For example, you might read *a* as 'a' in *apple* when you get the romanized Korean word *sam* (삼) 'three'; or you might read it as 'a' in *syllable* for either *a* in the romanized Korean word *saram* (사람) 'person', etc.

To avoid this type of confusion, some examples of English words containing sounds equivalent to some of the romanized Korean vowels and consonants are given as follows (approximate guideline only):

Vowels *eo, eu, ae* and *oe* are single vowels in romanized Korean as shown below. Therefore careful attention should be given to these vowels in not splitting them into two. Also, careful attention should be given to *u* [우] not to be read as English 'you'. Some common vowels which might confuse you are:

a	아	**ah**, f**a**ther	(but shorter)
eo	어	c**u**t, p**o**t	(but shorter)
o	오	b**a**ll, p**o**re	(but shorter)
u	우	sh**oe**, sch**oo**l	(but shorter)
eu	으	pronounced like the French word *euh*	
i	이	b**ee**, sh**ee**p	(but shorter)
ae	애	**a**pple, b**a**d	
e	에	b**e**d, **e**gg	
oe	외	w**e**t, w**e**lcome	

There won't be much trouble in pronouncing romanized Korean consonants except some tensed ones which require a relatively strong muscular effort in the vocal organs without the expulsion of air. Some examples are given as follow:

kk	ㄲ	s**k**i, s**k**y	(*k* after *s*)
tt	ㄸ	s**t**eak, s**t**ing	(*t* after *s*)
pp	ㅃ	s**p**eak, s**p**y	(*p* after *s*)
ss	ㅆ	**s**ea, **s**ir	(*s* before a vowel)
jj	ㅉ	bri**dg**e, mi**dg**et	(similar to a tutting sound in an exhaling way)

Basic grammar

1 Word order

Unlike in English, the Korean verb (action verb or adjectival verb) comes at the end of a sentence or clause. Also the Korean word order is quite flexible because there are special markers attached to the words in a sentence. They are called particles, and they mark the function of the words in a sentence: which word is a subject or an object etc. By contrast, in English you cannot simply change the word order in a sentence without violating its meaning because the position of words in a sentence tells us which is a subject or an object. One could not say, for example, 'A mouse chased the cat' to mean 'The cat chased a mouse'. In Korean, the meaning is clear irrespective of the position because of the particles affixed to the subject and the object: 'The cat-*ga* a mouse-*reul* chased' and 'A mouse-*reul* the cat-*ga* chased' (*ga* indicates 'the cat' is the subject, *reul* indicates 'a mouse' is the object).

2 Common particles

Some of the common particles are:

Subject marker: *i* (이) (after a word ending in a consonant), *ga* (가) (after a word ending in a vowel);
Topic/contrast marker: *eun* (은) (after a word ending in a consonant), *neun* (는) (after a word ending in a vowel);
Object marker: *eul* (을) (after a word ending in a consonant), *reul* (를) (after a word ending in a vowel);
Place/time marker (in/at/on) : *e* (에) (place marker *eseo* (에서) has a special usage but it is not covered here)

3 Leaving out the subject of a sentence

Although the subject comes at the beginning of the sentence, it is often omitted if it is clearly understood from the context by the participants in a conversation.

Where do you live?	*Eodi saseyo?*	(lit., where live?)
I live in Sydney	*Sidenie sarayo*	(lit., Sydney at live)
What are you doing?	*Mwo haeyo?*	(lit., what do?)
I am studying	*Gongbu haeyo*	(lit., study)

4 Action verbs and descriptive verbs

Korean adjectives conjugate like verbs, therefore they are often called adjectival verbs or descriptive verbs. To distinguish them from an adjectival or descriptive verbs, a normal verb is sometimes called an action verb.

You can see most of the adjectives in the dictionary of this book have two entries, one in a dictionary form which ends in *-da* (다) and the other in an adjectival form which modifies a noun in front of it. Verb conjugation is carried out by adding infixes or suffixes to the verb stem. The verb stem is the part of the verb remaining after *-da* (다) is taken away from the dictionary form of the verb.

5 Honorific language

When you speak Korean, you have to know who you are talking to. Depending on your relationship with them, their age and their social status, you have to choose an appropriate level of politeness when you talk. There are several speech levels in Korean. These speech levels are indicated in a sentence by the sentence-final suffixes attached to the end of verb stems. We will not cover all these levels here. We will only talk about the most common polite endings, which travelers are most likely to use in a real situation: formal polite form, informal polite form and informal honorific form.

Formal polite forms

This is used in formal situations, and is common in men's conversation. You add *-mnida* (ㅂ니다) if the verb stem ends in a vowel. Otherwise, you add *-seumnida* (습니다). If you want to make a question sentence, you simply change the final *-da* (다) of these formal polite verb-endings into *kka*? (까?).

Informal polite forms

This is common in daily conversation. This form requires a slightly more complicated process compared to the others. Firstly you have to look at the final vowel of the verb stem. If it is *a* (아) or *o* (오), you add *-ayo* (아요). Otherwise you add *-eoyo* (어요). If the verb stem ends in a vowel, you come to have two consecutive vowels after this conjugation. Two consecutive vowels will usually be fused into one. For example, *o* (오) and *a* (아) become *wa* (와). If the two consecutive vowels are the same vowel, one of them will be eliminated. If the verb stem ends in *eu* (으), which is the weakest vowel in Korean, it will also be eliminated.

There are a couple of exceptions to this conjugation rule. If the verb stem ends in *ha* (하), you always change this *ha* (하) into *haeyo* (해요). For the verb *ida* (이다) (to be: equation), you change this particular verb into *yeyo* (예요) after a word ending in a vowel. Otherwise you change this into *ieyo* (이에요). To make a question sentence, you simply say the same sentence with a rising tone at the end as you normally do in a question. There is no grammatical change between a statement and a question sentence when using this form.

Informal honorific forms

When you talk to the people clearly superior to you, such as your clients or guests, much older people or socially high-ranking people, you use an honorific form of language to show your respect to them. Of course you never use this form to refer to yourself. The process of this conjugation is quite simple. You add *-seyo* (세요) if the verb stem ends in a vowel. Otherwise, you add *-euseyo* (으세요).

Too many levels to work out which one to use? Don't panic! They are all polite forms at least. Whichever form you use, you are still in the range of common expectation from the native Korean speakers. Anyway, they often use a mixture of all these levels of language even in a conversation with the same person.

6 Some useful grammatical forms

The following grammatical items might help you to make new sentences as long as you know the words.

Would/Could you do something for me?
(*jom*) (좀) verb stem   +   *a/eo jusige sseoyo?* (아/어 주시겠어요?)

If the final vowel in the verb stem is *a* (아) or *o* (오), you choose *-a* (아). Otherwise you choose *-eo* (어). Please refer to the 'informal polite form' section for more details on how to conjugate verbs.

to fix,   *...jom gochyeo jusige sseoyo?*   Could you fix ...?
gochida, 고치다

| to find, *chatda*, 찾다 | *...jom chaja jusige sseoyo?* | Could you find ...?, |
| to see, *boda*, 보다 | *...jom bwa jusige sseoyo?* | Could you see ...? |

Please do something (for me)
(jom) (좀) verb stem   +   *a/eo juseyo?*   (아/어 주세요?)

Please refer to the above to see how you add -*a* (아) or -*o* (오).

to fix, *gochida*, 고치다	*...jom gochyeo juseyo?*	Please fix ...
to write down, *sseuda*, 쓰다	*...jom sseo juseyo?*	Please write ...down.
to see, *boda*, 보다	*...jom bwa juseyo?*	Please see ...

Don't do it, please
verb stem   +   *ji maseyo* (지 마세요)

to eat, *meokda*, 먹다	*...meokji maseyo*	Don't eat ..., please.
to smoke, *dambae piuda*, 담배 피우다	*dambae piuji maseyo*	Don't smoke, please.
to come, *oda*, 오다	*oji maseyo*	Don't come, please.

I want to do something
verb stem   +   *go sipeoyo* (고 싶어요)

to go, *gada*, 가다	*gago sipeoyo*	I want to go.
to see, *boda*, 보다	*...-reul/eul bogo sipeoyo*	I want to see ...
to buy, *sada*, 사다	*...-reul/eul sago sipeoyo*	I want to buy ...

1. The Basics

1.1   Personal details
1.2   Today or tomorrow?
1.3   What time is it?
1.4   One, two, three...
1.5   The weather
1.6   Here, there...
1.7   What does that sign say?
1.8   Legal holidays

1.1   Personal details

surname	*seong* 성
first name	*ireum* 이름
initials	*init syal* 이닛샬
address (street/number)	*juso (ga/beonji)* 주소 (가/번지)
postal code/town	*upyeon beonho/si* 우편번호/시
sex (male/female)	*seong (namseong/yeoseong)* 성 (남성/여성)
nationality	*gukjeok* 국적
date of birth	*saengnyeo nworil* 생년월일
place of birth	*chulsaengji* 출생지
occupation	*jigeop* 직업
marital status	*gyeolhon yeobu* 결혼 여부

married/single	*gihon/mihon* 기혼/미혼
widowed	*sabyeolhan* 사별한
(number of) children	*janyeo(su)* 자녀(수)
place and date of issue	*balhaeng gi gwan mit iljja* 발행 기관 및 일자
passport/identity card/ driving license number	*yeokkwon/sinbun jjeung/ unjeon myeon heo beonho* 여권/신분증/운전면허 번호
signature	*seomyeong* 서명

1.2 Today or tomorrow?

What day is it today?	*Oneureun museun yo iri eyo?* 오늘은 무슨 요일이에요?
Today's Monday.	*Oneureun woryo iri eyo.* 오늘은 월요일이에요.
– Tuesday	*Hwayo iri eyo* 화요일이에요
– Wednesday	*Suyo iri eyo* 수요일이에요
– Thursday	*Mogyo iri eyo* 목요일이에요
– Friday	*Geumyo iri eyo* 금요일이에요
– Saturday	*Toyo iri eyo* 토요일이에요
– Sunday	*Iryo iri eyo* 일요일이에요
in January	*irwo re* 일월에
since February	*iwo buteo* 이월부터

in spring	*bome*	
	봄에	
in summer	*yeo reume*	
	여름에	
in autumn	*ga eure*	
	가을에	
in winter	*gyeo ure*	
	겨울에	
2017	*icheon sibil lyeon*	
	이천십일 년	
the twenty-first century	*isibil segi*	
	이십일 세기	
What's the date today?	*Oneuri myeo chiri eyo?*	
	오늘이 몇일이에요?	
Today's the 24th.	*Oneureun isip sa iri eyo.*	
	오늘은 이십 사일이에요.	
Monday 3 November	*Sibi rwol sa mil, wo ryo iri eyo*	
	십일월 삼일, 월요일이에요	
in the morning	*achime*	
	아침에	
in the afternoon	*ohu e*	
	오후에	
in the evening	*jeonyeoge*	
	저녁에	
at night	*bame*	
	밤에	
this morning	*oneul achim*	
	오늘 아침	
this afternoon	*oneul ohu*	
	오늘 오후	
this evening	*oneul jyeo nyeok*	
	오늘 저녁	
tonight	*oneul bam*	
	오늘 밤	
last night	*eojet bam*	
	어제 밤	

this week	*ibeon ju* 이번 주
next.../next month	*...daeum/daeum dal* ...다음 다음 달
last year	*jang nyeon* 작년
in...days/weeks/ months/years	*...il/ju/dal/nyeon hu e* ...일/주/달/년 후에
...weeks ago	*...ju jeon* ...주 전
day off	*bibeon, swineun nal* 비번, 쉬는 날
yesterday	*eoje* 어제
tomorrow	*naeil* 내일

1.3 What time is it?

What time is it?	*Jigeum myeotsi yeyo?* 지금 몇 시예요?
It's nine o'clock.	*Ahop si eyo.* 아홉시에요.
– five past ten	*yeolsi obun ieyo* 열시 오분이에요
– a quarter past eleven	*yeolhansi sibobun ieyo* 열한시 십오분이에요
– twenty past twelve	*yeol dusi isipbun ieyo* 열두시 이십분이에요
– half past one	*hansi ban ieyo* 한시 반이에요
– twenty-five to three	*sesi isi bobun jeon ieyo* 세시 이십오분 전이에요
– a quarter to four	*nesi sibobun jeon ieyo* 네시 십오분 전이에요
– ten to five	*daseotsi sipbun jeon ieyo* 다섯시 십분 전이에요

It's midday (twelve noon).	*Jeongo(nat yeoldusi) eyo.* 정오(낮 열 두시)에요.
It's midnight.	*Jajeong(bam yeoldusi) ieyo.* 자정(밤 열 두시)이에요.
half an hour	*sam sipbun* 삼십분
What time?	*Myeot siyeyo?* 몇시예요?
What time can I come by?	*Myeot sie gamyeon dwaeyo?* 몇시에 가면 돼요?
at...	*...e* ...에
after...	*...hu e* ...후에
before...	*...jeone* ...전에
between...and...(o'clock)	*...sie seo...si sa ie* ...시에서...시 사이에
from...to...	*...buteo...kkaji* ...부터...까지
in...minutes	*...bun hu e* ...분 후에
– an hour	*hansigan hu e* 한시간 후에
– ...hours	*...sigan hu e* ...시간 후에
– a quarter of an hour	*sibobun hu e* 십 오분 후에
– three quarters of an hour	*sasi bobun hu e* 사십 오분 후에
too early/late	*neomu il jjik/neut ge* 너무 일찍/늦게
on time	*jeonggage* 정각에
summer time (daylight saving)	*sseomeo taim* 써머 타임

1.4 One, two, three...

0	*yeong* 영	17	*sipchil* 십칠
1	*il* 일	18	*sippal* 십팔
2	*i* 이	19	*sipgu* 십구
3	*sam* 삼	20	*isip* 이십
4	*sa* 사	21	*isibil* 이십일
5	*o* 오	22	*isibi* 이십이
6	*yuk* 육	30	*samsip* 삼십
7	*chil* 칠	31	*samsibil* 삼십일
8	*pal* 팔	32	*samsibi* 삼십이
9	*gu* 구	40	*sasip* 사십
10	*sip* 십	50	*osip* 오십
11	*sibil* 십일	60	*yuksip* 육십
12	*sibi* 십이	70	*chilsip* 칠십
13	*sipsam* 십삼	80	*palsip* 팔십
14	*sipsa* 십사	90	*gusip* 구십
15	*sibo* 십오	100	*baek* 백
16	*sim nyuk* 십육	101	*baegil* 백일

110	*baeksip* 백십	800	*palbaek* 팔백
120	*baegisip* 백이십	900	*gubaek* 구백
200	*ibaek* 이백	1,000	*cheon* 천
300	*sambaek* 삼백	1,100	*cheonbaek* 천백
400	*sabaek* 사백	2,000	*icheon* 이천
500	*obaek* 오백	10,000	*man* 만
600	*yukbaek* 육백	100,000	*sim man* 십 만
700	*chilbaek* 칠백	1,000,000	*baeng man* 백 만

1st *cheot beonjjae/cheotjjae*
첫 번째/첫째

2nd *du beonjjae/duljjae*
두 번째/둘째

3rd *se beonjjae/setjjae*
세 번째/셋째

4th *ne beonjjae/netjjae*
네 번째/넷째

5th *daseot beonjjae/daseot jjae*
다섯 번째/다섯째

6th *yeoseot beonjjae/yeoseot jjae*
여섯 번째/여섯째

7th *ilgop beonjjae/ilgop jjae*
일곱 번째/일곱째

8th *yeodeol beon jjae/yeodeol jjae*
여덟 번째/여덟째

9th *ahop beonjjae/ahop jjae*
아홉 번째/아홉째

10th *yeol beonjjae/yeol jjae*
열 번째/열째

11th	*yeol hanbeonjjae* 열 한번째		19th	*yeol ahop beonjjae* 열 아홉번째
12th	*yeol du beonjjae* 열 두번째		20th	*seumu beonjjae* 스무 번째
13th	*yeol se beonjjae* 열 세번째		21st	*seumul hanbeonjjae* 스물 한 번째
14th	*yeol ne beonjjae* 열 네번째		22nd	*seumul du beonjjae* 스물 두 번째
15th	*yeol daseot beonjjae* 열 다섯번째		30th	*seoreun beonjjae* 서른 번째
16th	*yeol yeoseot beonjjae* 열 여섯번째		100th	*baek beonjjae* 백 번째
17th	*yeol ilgop beonjjae* 열 일곱번째		1,000th	*cheon beonjjae* 천 번째
18th	*yeol yeodeol beonjjae* 열 여덟번째			

once	*han beon* 한 번		half	*ban* 반
twice	*du beon* 두 번		a quarter	*sabunui il* 사분의 일
double	*du bae* 두 배		a third	*sambunui il* 삼분의 일
triple	*se bae* 세 배		some/a few	*jogeum* 조금

$2 + 4 = 6$ *i deohagi saneun yuk*
이 더하기 사는 육

$4 - 2 = 2$ *sa bbaegi ineun i*
사 빼기 이는 이

$2 \times 4 = 8$ *i gopagi saneun pal*
이 곱하기 사는 팔

$4 \div 2 = 2$ *sa nanugi ineun i*
사 나누기 이는 이

even/odd	*jjaksu/holsu*
	짝수/홀수
total	*hap(gye)*
	합(계)
6 x 9	*yuk gopagi gu*
	육 곱하기 구

1.5 The weather

Is the weather going to be good/bad?	*Nalssiga joeul/nappeul geoyeyeo?*
	날씨가 좋을/나쁠 거예요?
Is it going to get colder/hotter?	*Nalssiga chuul/deo ul geoyeyeo?*
	날씨가 추울/더울 거예요?
What temperature is it going to be?	*Gioni eolmana doel geoyeyeo?*
	기온이 얼마나 될 거예요?
Is it going to rain?	*Biga ol geoyeyeo?*
	비가 올 거예요?
Is there going to be a storm?	*Pokpungi ol geoyeyeo?*
	폭풍이 올 거예요?
Is it going to snow?	*Nuni ol geoyeyeo?*
	눈이 올 거예요?
Is it going to freeze?	*Gili eoleul geoyeyeo?*
	길이 얼을 거예요?
Is the thaw setting in?	*Nokgi sija kheyo?*
	녹기 시작해요?
Is it going to be foggy?	*Angaega kkil geoyeyeo?*
	안개가 낄 거예요?
Is there going to be a thunderstorm?	*Cheondungi chil geoyeyeo?*
	천둥이 칠 거예요?
The weather's changing.	*Nalssiga ba kkwigo itseoyo.*
	날씨가 바뀌고 있어요.
It's going to be cold.	*Nari chuweojil geoyeyo.*
	날이 추워질 거예요.
What's the weather going to be like today/tomorrow?	*Oneul/naeil nalssineun eotteol geoyeyeo?*
	오늘/내일 날씨는 어떨 거예요?

sweltering/muggy *mudeoun* 무더운	sunny *hwachanghan* 화창한	rain *bi* 비
sunny day *kwaecheonghan nal* 쾌청한 날	windy *balam buneun* 바람 부는	heavy rain *pogu* 폭우
cool *seoneulhan/siwonhan* 서늘한/시원한	ice/icy *eol eum/gili eon* 얼음/길이 언	wind *balam* 바람
very hot *maeu deoun* 매우더운	cloudiness *guleumi kkin/heulin* 구름이 낀/흐린	snow *nun* 눈
clear skies/cloudy/overcast *malg eun/guleum kkin/ jantteug heulin haneul* 맑은/구름 낀/잔뜩 흐린 하늘	frost/frosty *ssal/ssalhan* 쌀/쌀한	frost *seoli* 서리
hurricane *heoli kein/taepung* 허리케인/태풍	overnight frost *bam seoli* 밤 서리	downpour *pogu/hou* 폭우/호우
...degrees (below/above zero) *do(yeongha/yeongsang)* ...도(영하/영상)	gusts of wind *gangpung* 강풍	heatwave *hog seo* 혹서
moderate/strong/ very strong winds *jeogdanghan/ganghan/ maeu ganghan balam* 적당한/강한/매우 강한 바람	storm *pogpung* 폭풍	mild *onhwahan* 온화한
fog/foggy *angae/angaega jaughan* 안개/안개가 자욱한	cold and damp *chubgo seubhan* 춥고 습한	hail *ubag* 우박
stifling *summag hige deoun* 숨막히게 더운	humid *nugnughan/seubhan* 눅눅한/습한	fine/clear *malg eun* 맑은
	bleak *euseu seuhan* 으스스한	

1.6 Here, there...

See also 5.1 Asking directions

here, over here/there, over there	*yeogi/jeogi* 여기/저기
somewhere/nowhere	*eodin gae/amu dedo* 어딘가에/아무데도
everywhere	*eodi e na* 어디에나
far away/nearby	*meolli/gakka ie(geuncheoe)* 멀리/가까이에(근처에)
(on the) right/ (on the) left	*oreun jjok/oen jjok* 오른쪽/왼쪽
to the right/left of	*oreun jjogro/oen jjogro* 오른쪽으로/왼쪽으로
straight ahead	*baro ap* 바로 앞
via	*...reul jina* ...를 지나
in	*...ane* ...안에
to	*...ro* ...로
on	*...wi e* ...위에
under	*...arae* ...아래
opposite/facing	*majeun pyeone* 맞은 편에
next to	*...yeope* ...옆에
near	*...geuncheoe* ...근처에
in front of/at the front	*...ape* ...앞에

The Basics

1

in the center	*gaunde e* 가운데에	
forward	*apeuro* 앞으로	
up/down	*wiro/araero* 위로/아래로	
inside	*anui/ane* 안의/안에	
outside	*bakkat jjogui/bakkat jjoge* 바깥쪽의/바깥쪽에	
behind/at the back	*dwi e* 뒤에	
in the north	*bukjjo ge* 북쪽에	
to the south	*namjjo geuro* 남쪽으로	
from the west	*seojjo geseo* 서쪽에서	
from the east	*dongjjo geseo* 동쪽에서	
to the...of	*ui...jjo geuro* 의…쪽으로	

1.7 What does that sign say?

See 5.2 Traffic signs

For Hire *Daeyeo* 대여	Hotel *Hotel* 호텔	Traffic Police *Gyotong Sunyeong* 교통 순경
Sold Out *Maejin* 매진	Out of Order *Gojang* 고장	Fire Department *Sobangseo* 소방서
Waiting Room *Daegisil* 대기실	Stop *Jeongji* 정지	(Municipal) Police *(Silib) Gyeongchal* (시립) 경찰

Information
Annae
안내

Open
Yeongeob Jung
영업 중

Pull
Dang Gisio
당기시오

Push
Misio
미시오

Emergency Exit
Bisang Gu
비상구

Not in Use
Sayong Geumji
사용 금지

Admission (Free)
Ibjang (Mulyo)
입장 (무료)

Hot/Cold Water
Onsu/Naengsu
온수/냉수

Bathrooms
Hwajangsil
화장실

Wet Paint
Peinteu Juui
페인트 주의

Drinking Water
Sigsu
식수

Danger
Wiheom
위험

For Rent
Se Noheum
세 놓음

For Sale
Maemul
매물

Post Office
Uchegug
우체국

Entrance
Ibgu
입구

Ticket Office
Maepyoso
매표

Closed
Mun Dad Eum
문 닫음

Full
Man Won
만원

Reserved
Yeyagseog
예약석

Police
Gyeongchal
경찰

Hospital
Byeong Won
병원

Exchange
Hwanjeon
환전

Timetable
Unhaengpyo
운행표

Cashier
Hyeongeum Chulnab Won
현금 출납원

Danger/Fire Hazard
Wiheom/Hwajae Wiheom
위험/화재 위험

Emergency Brake
Bisang Jedong jangchi
비상 제동장치

No Smoking/No Litter
Geumyeon/Sseulegi Tugi Geumji
금연/쓰레기 투기 금지

No Access/No Entry
Jeobgeun Geumji/Chul Ibgeumji
접근 금지/출입금지

First Aid/Accident And Emergency (Hospital)
Eung Geub Cheochi
응급 처치

Please Do Not Disturb/Touch
Sondaeji Masio
손대지 마시오

Fire Escape/Escalator
Hwajaesi Talchulgu/ Eseuke olleiteo
화재시 탈출구/ 에스칼레이터

No Hunting/Fishing
Sanyang/Nakksi Geumji
사냥/낚시 금지

Tourist Information Bureau
Gwangwang Annaeso
관광 안내소

Engaged (In Use)	High Voltage
Sayong Jung	*Goab*
사용 중	고압

1.8 Legal holidays

National holidays in Korea are:

January 1: New Year's Day *Saehae Cheotnal* 새해 첫날

January–February: Korean New Year (Lunar) *Seolnal* 설날
This falls on the first day of the Korean Lunar Calendar, and the celebrations usually last three days- the eve of the first day, and the first and second day of the calendar. This festival is a time to respect their ancestors and to catch up with distant family members. Expect delays on roads and elevated transport ticket prices.

March 1: Samil Independence Movement Day *Samiljeol* 삼일절
This celebrates the independence movement in 1919 against Japanese colonial rule. There will be a reading of the declaration at Tapgol Park in Seoul in a special ceremony.

April: Buddha's Birthday (Lunar) *Seok Katan Sinil* 석가탄신일
This day—on the eighth day of the fourth lunar month—celebrates the birth of Buddha; on the eve, a street parade with multi-colored lanterns is held.

May 5: Children's Day *Eori Ninal* 어린이날
A day dedicated for parents to spend time with their children in fun-filled recreational activities.

June 6: Memorial Day *Hyeonchungil* 현충일
This day pays tribute to those who sacrificed their lives for the country. Visit the National Cemetery in Seoul to see the ceremony.

August 15: Liberation Day *Gwangbokjeol* 광복절
  This day celebrates Korea's liberation following Japan's surrender to the Allied forces in 1945.

August: Thanksgiving Day (Lunar) *Chuseok* 추석
  Chuseok, which happens on the 15th day of the lunar calendar, is the most important traditional holiday. During these three days, everyone heads back to their hometown, so heavy traffic congestion on major highways should be expected during these days.

October 3: National Foundation Day *Gaecheonjeol* 개천절
  The holiday celebrates the forming of the first Korean state, Gojoseon, in 2333 BC. By extension, this date is also traditionally regarded as the date the Korean nation was founded.

December 25: Christmas Day *Seongtanjeol* 성탄절
  Unlike in Japan, Christmas Day in South Korea is recognized as an official public holiday, and churches will be decorated with lights. Increasingly, attending church for Christmas services is popular, even among non-Christians.

2. Meet and Greet

2.1 **Greetings**
2.2 **Asking a question**
2.3 **How to reply**
2.4 **Thank you**
2.5 **I'm sorry**
2.6 **What do you think?**

Koreans greet each other with a bow. Younger people should bow deeply to show their respect to the elderly. Handshakes are exchanged among adults, but are less acceptable when greeting a woman.

2.1 Greetings

Good morning/ afternoon/evening.	*Annyeong haseyo.* 안녕하세요.
Hello Peter, how are things?	*Annyeong haseyo Piteossi.* *Jal doeseyo?* 안녕하세요 피터씨. 잘 되세요?
Hi Helen; fine, thank you, and you?	*Ne Helenssi. Annyeong haseyo?* 네 헬렌씨 안녕하세요?
Very well, and you?	*Ne eoddeokke jinae seyo?* 네 어떻게 지내세요?
In excellent health/ In great shape	*Ne jalji naeyo* 네 잘지내요
So-so	*Geujeo geuraeyo* 그저 그래요
Not very well	*Aju jochineun anneyo* 아주 좋지는 않네요
Not bad	*Geunyang jinaeyo* 그냥 지내요
I'm going to leave.	*Gabwaya gesseoyo.* 가봐야겠어요.
I have to be going, someone's waiting for me.	*Jigeum nuga gida rigo isseoseo gaya gesseoyo.* 지금 누가 기다리고 있어서 가야겠어요.

29

Goodbye.	**Annyeonghi gaseyo.** 안녕히 가세요.
See you later.	**Tto bwayo.** 또 봐요.
See you soon.	**Dasi bwayo.** 다시 봐요.
See you in a little while.	**Jomangan dasi bwayo.** 조만간 다시 봐요.
Sweet dreams.	**Jal jayo.** 잘 자요.
Good night.	**Annyeonghi jumuseyo.** 안녕히 주무세요.
All the best/Have fun.	**Jal jinae seyo.** 잘 지내세요.
Good luck.	**Haenguneul bireoyo.** 행운을 빌어요.
Have a nice vacation.	**Huga jal bonae seyo.** 휴가 잘 보내세요.
Bon voyage/Have a good trip.	**Yeohaeng jal danyeo oseyo.** 여행 잘 다녀 오세요.
Thank you, the same to you.	**Goma woyo, jal jinae seyo.** 고마워요, 잘 지내세요.
Say hello to/Give my regards to...	**...ege anbu jeonhae juseyo** ...에게 안부 전해 주세요

2.2 Asking a question

Who/Who's that?/ Who is it?/Who's there?	**Nugu?/Nugu seyo?** 누구/누구세요?
What?	**Mwoyeoyo?** 뭐예요?
What is there to see?	**Bol gesi innayo?** 볼 것이 있나요?
What category of hotel is it?	**Museun geup hoteri eyo?** 무슨 급 호텔이에요?

Where?	*Eodi eyo?*
	어디예요?
Where's the bathroom?	*Hwajang siri eodi eyo?*
	화장실이 어디예요?
Where are you going?	*Eodi gaseyo?*
	어디 가세요?
Where are you from?	*Eodiseo wasseoyo?*
	어디서 왔어요?
How far is that?	*Eolmana meoreoyo?*
	얼마나 멀어요?
How long does that take?	*Eolmana geollyeoyo?*
	얼마나 걸려요?
How long is the trip?	*Yeohaengeun eolmana geolli nayo?*
	여행은 얼마나 걸리나요?
How much/	*Eolma yeyo?/Igeo eolma yeyo?*
How much is this?	얼마예요/이거 얼마예요?
What time is it?	*Myeot siyeyo?*
	몇 시예요?
Which one/s?	*Eoneu geot?*
	어느 것?
Which glass is mine?	*Eoneu keobi naekkeo yeyo?*
	어느 컵이 내거예요?
When/When are	*Eonjeyo/Eonje ddeonayo?*
you leaving?	언제요/언제 떠나요?
Why/Why are	*Waeyo/Wae gaseyo?*
you leaving?	왜요/왜 가세요?
Could you...?	*...ayeo juseyo?*
	알려주세요
Could you help me/	*(Jom) dowa juseyo?*
give me a hand please?	(좀) 도와주세요?
Could you come with	*Gachi jom ga juseyo?*
me, please?	같이 좀 가 주세요?
Could you reserve/book	*Yeyak jom hae juseyo?*
me some tickets please?	예약 좀 해 주세요?
Could you recommend	*Dareun hotereul jom allyeo juseyo?*
another hotel?	다른 호텔을 좀 알려주세요?

Could you point that out to me/show me please?	*Eotteoke ganeunji gareuchyeo juseyo?* 어떻게 가는지 가르쳐 주세요?
Do you know…/Do you know whether…?	*…aseyo?/…inji aseyo?* …아세요?/…인지 아세요?
Do you have…?/Do you have a … for me?	*…isseoyo?/Isseu seyo?* …있어요?/…있으세요?
Do you have a vegetarian dish, please?	*Chaesik doeanyo?* 채식 되나요?
I would like…	*…juseyo* 주세요
I'd like a kilo of apples, please.	*Sagwa il killo juseyo.* 사과 일 킬로 주세요.
Can/May I?	*…dwaeyo?* …돼요?
Can/May I take this away?	*Igeo gajyeo gado dwaeyo?* 이거 가져가도 돼요?
Can I smoke here?	*Yeogiseo dambae piwodo dwaeyo?* 여기서 담배 피워도 돼요?
Could I ask you something?	*Mwo jom mureo bwado dwaeyo?* 뭐 좀 물어봐도 돼요?

2.3 How to reply

Yes, of course.	*Ne, mullo nijyo.* 네, 물론이죠.
No, I'm sorry.	*Joesong hajiman an dwaeyo.* 죄송하지만 안 돼요.
Yes, what can I do for you?	*Ne, mwol dowa dril kkayo?* 네 뭘 도와드릴까요?
Just a moment, please.	*Jamsi manyo.* 잠시만요.
No, I don't have time now.	*Aniyo, jigeum sigani eobseoyo.* 아니오, 지금 시간이 없어요.
No, that's impossible.	*Aniyo, andwaeyo.* 아니오, 안돼요.

I think so/I think that's absolutely right.	*Ne, majayo.* 네, 맞아요.
I think so too/I agree.	*Jeodo geureoke saengga kaeyo.* 저도 그렇게 생각해요.
I agree/don't agree.	*Ne geuraeyo/geureochi anayo.* 네 그래요/그렇지 않아요.
OK/it's fine.	*Ne, joayo.* 네, 좋아요.
OK, all right.	*Ne, dwaess seoyo.* 네, 됐어요.
I hope so too.	*Geurae sseumyeon jo ke sseoyo.* 그랬으면 좋겠어요.
No, not at all/ Absolutely not.	*Jeonhyeo anieyo/jeoldaero ani eyo.* 전혀 아니에요/절대로 아니에요.
No, no one.	*Aniyo, amu doyo.* 아니오, 아무도요.
No, nothing.	*Aniyo, amu geotdo ani eyo.* 아니오, 아무것도 아니에요.
That's right.	*Majayo.* 맞아요.
Something's wrong.	*Mwoga jal mot dwaesseoyo.* 뭐가 잘 못 됐어요.
Perhaps/maybe.	*Ama doyo.* 아마도요.
I don't know.	*Jal moreu gesseoyo.* 잘 모르겠어요.

2.4 Thank you

Thank you.	*Goma woyo.* 고마워요.
Thank you for...	*...haejwoseo goma woyo* ...해줘서 고마워요
Thank you very much.	*Gamsa hamnida.* 감사합니다.

You shouldn't have.	*Ireoke kkaji hae jusyeoseo gamsa hamnida.* 이렇게까지 해주셔서 감사합니다.
I enjoyed it very much.	*Jeulgeo wosseoyo.* 즐거웠어요.
You're welcome/ That's all right.	*Gwenchan tayo/ani eyo.* 괜찮아요/아니에요.
My pleasure/ don't mention it.	*Beol malsseu meulyo.* 별 말씀을요.
Excuse me (starting to speak to a stranger).	*Sillye hamnida.* 실례합니다.

2.5 I'm sorry

Excuse me/pardon me (ask to repeat what's been said)?	*Mworago hasyeo sseoyo?* 뭐라고 하셨어요?
I do apologize.	*Sagwa deuryeoyo.* 사과 드려요.
I'm sorry/I didn't know that...	*Joesong haeyo/...molla sseoyo* 죄송해요/...몰랐어요
I didn't mean it/It was an accident.	*Ilbureo geureon geon ani eyo.* 일부러 그런 건 아니에요.
That's all right/Don't worry about it.	*Gwaencha nayo/geokjeong maseyo.* 괜찮아요/걱정 마세요.
Never mind/Forget it.	*Amu ildo ani eyo.* 아무 일도 아니에요.
It could happen to anyone.	*Geureol sudo itjyo.* 그럴 수도 있죠.

2.6 What do you think?

| Which do you prefer/
like best? | *Eotteon ge deo joayo?*
어떤 게 더 좋아요? |
| What do you think? | *Eotteoke saenggak haseyo?*
어떻게 생각하세요? |

Don't you like dancing?	*Chum chuneun geo joa haji aneu seyo?* 춤 추는 거 좋아하지 않으세요?
I don't mind.	*Sanggwan eobseoyo.* 상관없어요.
Great/Wonderful!	*Hullyung haeyo/joayo!* 훌륭해요/좋아요!
I'm very happy/glad that/ delighted to...	*...haeseo joayo* ...해서 좋아요
It's really nice here	*Yeogi cham jonneyo.* 여기 참 좋네요.
How nice for you!	*Cham jal dwaess gunyo!* 참 잘 됐군요!
I'm (not) very happy with...	*...ga joayo/sireoyo* ...가 좋아요/싫어요
I'm having a great time.	*Jaemi isseoyo.* 재미있어요.
I can't wait till/I'm looking forward to tomorrow.	*Ppalli naeiri wasseumyeon jo ke sseoyo.* 빨리 내일이 왔으면 좋겠어요.
I hope it works out.	*Jal dwae sseumyeon jo ke sseoyo.* 잘 됐으면 좋겠어요.
How awful!/What a pity!/ What a shame!	*Jeoreon!* 저런!
What nonsense/How silly/ That's ridiculous!	*Maldo andwaeyo!* 말도 안돼요!
How disgusting!	*Jeongmal kkeum ji kaeyo!* 정말 끔찍해요!
I don't like it/them.	*Maeume andeu reyo.* 마음에 안 들어요
I'm fed up/bored.	*Jigyeo woyo.* 지겨워요.
This is no good.	*Igeon andwaeyo.* 이건 안 돼요.
This is not what I expected.	*Igeon ani jiyo.* 이건 아니지요.

3. Small Talk

3.1   Introductions
3.2   I beg your pardon?
3.3   Starting/ending a conversation
3.4   A chat about the weather
3.5   Hobbies
3.6   Invitations
3.7   Paying a compliment
3.8   Intimate comments/questions
3.9   Congratulations and condolences
3.10 Arrangements
3.11 Being the host(ess)
3.12 Saying goodbye

3.1   Introductions

May I introduce myself?	*Je sogereul halkkeyo?* 제 소개를 할게요?
My name's…	*Jei reumeun…imnida* 제 이름은…입니다
I'm…	*Jeoneun…imnida* 저는…입니다
What's your name?	*Ireumi mwoyeyo?* 이름이 뭐예요?
May I introduce…?	*…reul soge halkkeyo?* …를 소개할게요?
This is my wife/husband.	*Je anae/nampyeon ieyo.* 제 아내/남편이에요.
This is my daughter/son.	*Je ttar/adeul imnida.* 제 딸/아들입니다.
This is my mother/father.	*Je eomeoni/abeoji simnida.* 제 어머니/아버지이십니다.
This is my fiancée/fiancé.	*Je yakonnyeo/yakon jaeyo.* 제 약혼녀/약혼자에요.

This is my friend.	*Je chingu yeyo.* 제 친구예요.
How do you do?	*Manaseo banga woyo?* 만나서 반가워요?
Hi, pleased to meet you.	*Annyeong haseyo, manaseo banga woyo.* 안녕하세요, 만나서 반가워요.
Pleased to meet you.	*Manaseo bangap seumnida.* 만나서 반갑습니다.
Where are you from?	*Eodiseo wasseoyo?* 어디서 왔어요?
I'm American.	*Miguge seoyo.* 미국에서요.
What city do you live in?	*Eoneu dosie sarayo?* 어느 도시에 살아요?
in…near…	*…geuncheo …e sarayo* …근처…에 살아요
Have you been here long?	*Yeogi orae isseo sseoyo?* 여기 오래 있었어요?
A few days.	*Myeo chil isseo sseoyo.* 며칠 있었어요.
How long are you staying here?	*Yeogi eolmana orae gyesil geoeyo?* 여기 얼마나 오래 계실 거에요?
We're (probably) leaving tomorrow/in two weeks.	*(A ma) naeil/i ju hu e tteonal geoeyo.* (아마) 내일/이 주 후에 떠날 거에요.
Where are you staying?	*Eodi e gyeseyo?* 어디에 계세요?
I'm staying in a hotel/ an apartment.	*Hotere/apa teue isseoyo.* 호텔에/아파트에 있어요.
At a campsite.	*Yayeong jange.* 야영장에.
I'm staying with friends/relatives.	*Chingudeul/chincheokdeul hago gachi isseoyo.* 친구들/친척들하고 같이 있어요.
Are you here on your own?	*Yeogi e honja isseoyo?* 여기에 혼자 있어요?

Are you here with your family?	*Gajokgwa hamkke isseoyo?* 가족과 함께 있어요?
I'm on my own.	*Honja isseoyo.* 혼자 있어요.
I'm with my wife/ husband.	*Anae/nampyeongwa gachi isseoyo.* 아내/남편과 같이 있어요.
– with my family	*gajokkwa gachi isseoyo* 가족과 같이 있어요
– with relatives	*chincheo khago isseoyo* 친척하고 있어요
– with a friend/friends	*chingu(deul) gwa gachi isseoyo* 친구(들)과 같이 있어요
Are you married?	*Gyeolhon haesseoyo?* 결혼 했어요?
Are you engaged?	*Yakhon haesseoyo?* 약혼 했어요?
That's none of your business.	*Sanggwan maseyo.* 상관 마세요.
I'm married.	*Gyeolhon haesseoyo.* 결혼 했어요.
I'm single/not married.	*Miho nieyo/Gyeolhon an haesseoyo.* 미혼이에요/결혼 안 했어요.
I'm separated.	*Byeolgeo jung ieyo.* 별거 중이에요.
I'm divorced.	*Ihon haesseoyo.* 이혼했어요.
I'm a widow/widower.	*Honja dwaesseoyo.* 혼자됐어요.
Do you have any children/grandchildren?	*Janyeoneun eotteoke doeseyo/ sonjaneun innayo?* 자녀는 어떻게 되세요/손자는 있나요?
How old are you?	*Myeot sarieyo?* 몇 살이에요?
How old is she/he?	*Geu sarameun myeot sari eyo?* 그 사람은 몇 살이에요?

I'm…(years old).	...sari eyo …살이에요
She's/he's…(years old).	Geu sarameun...sari eyo. 그 사람은…살이에요.
What do you do for a living?	Museunil haseyo? 무슨 일 하세요?
I work in an office.	Samu sireseo ilhaeyo. 사무실에서 일해요.
I'm a student.	Haksaeng ieyo. 학생이에요.
I'm unemployed.	Il anhaeyo. 일 안 해요.
I'm retired.	Euntoe haesseoyo. 은퇴했어요.
I'm on a disability pension.	Jangaein yeongeum badayo. 장애인 연금 받아요.
I'm a housewife.	Gajeong jubu yeyo. 가정 주부예요.
Do you like your job?	Jikjang ili maeume deureoyo? 직장일이 마음에 들어요?
Most of the time.	Daebubun eunyo. 대부분은요.
Mostly I do, but I prefer vacations.	Ildo joa hajiman, hugaga deo joayo. 일도 좋아하지만, 휴가가 더 좋아요.

3.2 I beg your pardon?

I don't speak any/ I speak a little…	...mareun jeonhyeo/jogeum bakke moteyo …말은 전혀/조금밖에 못해요
Do you speak English?	Yeongeo hal jjul aseyo? 영어 할 줄 아세요?
Is there anyone who speaks…?	...mal hal jjul aneun saram isseoyo? …말 할 줄 아는 사람 있어요?

I beg your pardon/What?	*Mworago haesseoyo?* 뭐라고 했어 요?
I don't understand.	*Jal moreuge sseoyo.* 잘 모르겠어요.
Do you understand me?	*Alge sseoyo?* 알겠어요?
Could you repeat that, please?	*Dasi malsseumhae juseyo?* 다시 말씀해 주세요?
Could you speak more slowly, please?	*Cheoncheonhi malsseumhae juseyo?* 천천히 말씀해 주세요?
What does that mean?	*Geuge museun tteusi eyo?* 그게 무슨 뜻이에요?
What does that word mean?	*Geu danega museun tteusi eyo?* 그 단어가 무슨 뜻이에요?
It's more or less the same as...	*...wa biseut haeyo* ...와 비슷해요
Could you write that down for me, please?	*Geugeol jeogeo jusige sseoyo?* 그걸 적어 주시겠어요?
Could you spell that for me, please?	*Cheoljarol malhae juseyo?* 철자로 말해 주세요?
Could you point that out in this phrase book, please?	*I chaek eodi e jeokyeo inneunji gareuchyeo juseyo?* 이 책 어디에 적혀 있는지 가르쳐 주세요?
Just a minute, I'll look it up.	*Jamkkan manyo, chajabol kkeyo.* 잠깐만요, 찾아 볼게요.
I can't find the word/ the sentence.	*Geu daneoreul/munjangeul chajeul su eopseoyo.* 그 단어를/문장을 찾을 수 없어요.
How do you say that in...?	*...mallo geugeon eoddeokke malha nayo?* ...말로 그건 어떻게 말하나요?
How do you pronounce that?	*Eotteoke bareum hanayo?* 어떻게 발음하나요?

3.3 Starting/ending a conversation

Could I ask you something?	*Mwo jom mureo bwado dwaeyo?* 뭐 좀 물어봐도 돼요?
Excuse me.	*Sillye hamnida.* 실례합니다.
Could you help me please?	*Jom dowa jusige sseoyo?* 좀 도와주시겠어요?
Yes, what's the problem?	*Ne, museu niri seyo?* 네, 무슨 일이세요?
Sorry, I don't have time now.	*Joesong haeyo, jigeum sigani eopseoyo.* 죄송해요, 지금 시간이 없어요.
What can I do for you?	*Mwol dowajul gayo?* 뭘 도와줄까요?
Do you have a light?	*Bul jom billil su isseul kkayo?* 불 좀 빌릴 수 있을까요?
May I join you?	*Gachi haedo dwaeyo?* 같이 해도 돼요?
Could you take a picture of me/us?	*Sajin jom jjigeo jullaeyo?* 사진 좀 찍어 줄래요?
Leave me alone.	*Honja itge hae juseyo.* 혼자 있게 해주세요.
Go away or I'll scream.	*Jeori gaseyo angeu reomyeon sori jireul geoeyo.* 저리 가세요 안 그러면 소리지를 거에요.

3.4 A chat about the weather

See also 1.5 The weather

It's so hot/cold today!	*Oneul cham deowoyo/chuwoyo!* 오늘 참 더워요/추워요!
Isn't it a lovely day?	*Nalssi cham jochi anayo?* 날씨 참 좋지 않아요?
It's so windy/what a storm!	*Barami jeongmal mani buneyo!* 바람이 정말 많이 부네요!

All that rain/snow!	*Dawdanhan bi/nuniya!* 대단한 비/눈야!
It's so foggy!	*Angaega ja u kaeyo!* 안개가 자욱해요!
Has the weather been like this for long?	*Nalssiga oraet dongan iraen nayo?* 날씨가 오랫동안 이랬나요?
Is it always this hot/ cold here?	*Yeogin hangsang ireoke deoun gayo/chuun gayo?* 여긴 항상 이렇게 더운가요/추운가요?
Is it always this dry/ humid here?	*Yeogin hangsang ireoke geonjohan gayo/seuphan gayo?* 여긴 항상 이렇게 건조한가요/습한가요?

3.5 Hobbies

Do you have any hobbies?	*Museun chwimiga isseu seyo?* 무슨 취미가 있으세요?
I like knitting/ reading/photography.	*Tteugaejil/chae gilkki/sajin jjikgireul joa haeyo.* 뜨개질/책 읽기/사진 찍기를 좋아해요.
I enjoy listening to music.	*Eumak deunneun geol joa haeyo.* 음악 듣는 걸 좋아해요.
I play the guitar/ the piano.	*Gitareul/piano reul cheoyo.* 기타를/피아노를 쳐요.
I like the cinema.	*Yeonghwareul joa haeyo.* 영화를 좋아해요.
I like traveling/playing sports/going fishing/ going for a walk.	*Yeohaeng/undong/nak ssi/ sanchaegeul joa haeyo.* 여행/운동/낚시/산책을 좋아해요.
Korean drama/pop music is popular in other countries.	*Hanguk dramaga/daejungeu magi oeguk eso ingiga iseoyo.* 한국 드라마가/대중음악이 외국에서 인기가 있어요.
I am a fan of the figure skater "Yuna Kim."	*Figure seonsu "Kim Yuna" ui fan ieyo.* 피겨 선수 "김연아"의 팬이에요.
My hobby is playing computer games.	*Computer geimi je chwimi yeyo.* 컴퓨터 게임이 제 취미예요.

I listen to Korean pop a lot on my mp3 player/. handphone.	*Hanguk eumageul mp3 player/ haendeupon romani deureoyo.* 한국 음악을 mp3 플레이어로/핸드폰 많이 들어요.

3.6 Invitations

Would you like to go dancing with me?	*Jeowa hamkke chumchureo gasil laeyo?* 저와 함께 춤추러 가실래요?
Would you like to have lunch/dinner with me?	*Jeowa hamkke jeomsim/jeonyeok deusil laeyo?* 저와 함께 점심/저녁 드실래요?
Would you like to go out with me?	*Jeowa hamkke oechul hallaeyo?* 저와 함께 외출 할래요?
Would you like to come to the beach with me?	*Jeowa gachi haebyeo ne gasil laeyo?* 저와 같이 해변에 가실래요?
Would you like to come into town with us?	*Uri hago sinae e ga sil lae yo?* 우리하고 시내에 가실래요?
Would you like to come see some friends with us?	*Gachi chingu mannareo gallaeyo?* 같이 친구 만나러 갈래요?
Shall we dance?	*Chum chusil kkayo?* 춤 추실까요?
– sit at the bar?	*Bae anjeul kkayo?* 바에 앉을까요?
– get something to drink?	*Masil kkayo?* 마실까요?
– go for a walk/drive?	*Sanchae kareo/deura ibeu galkkayo?* 산책하러/드라이브 갈까요?
Yes, all right.	*Ne, joayo.* 네, 좋아요.
Good idea.	*Joeun saengga gieyo.* 좋은 생각이에요.
No thank you.	*Gomap jiman sayang halkkeyo.* 고맙지만 사양할께요.

Maybe later.	*Najung eyo.* 나중에요.
I don't feel like it.	*Byeollo naekiji anayo.* 별로 내키지 않아요.
I don't have time.	*Sigani eopseoyo.* 시간이 없어요.
I already have a date.	*Deiteu ga isseoyo.* 데이트가 있어요.
You look great.	*Geunsa handeyo.* 근사한데요.
I'm not very good at dancing/volleyball/ swimming.	*Chumeul jal mot chwoyo/baegureul jal mot haeyo/suyeongeul jal mot haeyo.* 춤을 잘 못 춰요/배구를 잘 못 해요/ 수영을 잘 못해요.

3.7 Paying a compliment

I like your car.	*Chaga cham jonneyo.* 차가 참 좋네요.
I like your ski outfit.	*Seuki jangbiga cham jonneyo.* 스키 장비가 참 좋네요.
You are very nice.	*Dangsin cham joeun sarami eyo.* 당신 참 좋은 사람이에요.
What a good boy/girl!	*Jeongmal chakagu nyo!* 정말 착하군요!
You're a good dancer.	*Chumeul jal chuneyo.* 춤을 잘 추네요.
You're a very good cook.	*Yorireul aju jal haneyo.* 요리를 아주 잘 하네요.
You're a good soccer player.	*Chukgureul aju jal haneyo.* 축구를 아주 잘 하네요.
I like being with you.	*Dangsin hago gachi inneunge joayo.* 당신하고 같이 있는 게 좋아요.

3.8 Intimate comments/questions

I've missed you so much.	*Jeongmal bogo sipeo sseoyo.* 정말 보고 싶었어요.
I dreamt about you.	*Dangsin e daehae kkumeul kkwosseoyo.* 당신에 대해 꿈을 꿨어요.
I think about you all day.	*Haru jongil dangsin saenggageul haeyo.* 하루 종일 당신 생각을 해요.
I've been thinking about you all day.	*Haru jongil dangsin saenggageul haesseoyo.* 하루 종일 당신 생각을 했어요.
You have such a sweet smile.	*Dangsine misoga jeongmal areumda woyo.* 당신의 미소가 정말 아름다워요.
You have such beautiful eyes.	*Dangsine nuni jeong mal areumda woyo.* 당신의 눈이 정말 아름다워요.
I'm in love with you/ I love you.	*Sarang haeyo.* 사랑해요.
I'm in love with you too	*Nado sarang haeyo.* 나도 사랑해요.
I love you too.	*Jeodoyo.* 저도요.
I don't feel as strongly about you.	*Dangsine daehae byeoldareun neukkimi eopseoyo.* 당신에 대해 별다른 느낌이 없어요.
I already have a girlfriend/boyfriend.	*Jeon imi yeoja chingu/namja chinguga isseoyo.* 전 이미 여자친구/남자친구가 있어요.
I'm not ready for that.	*Ajikeun an dwaeyo.* 아직은 안 돼요.
I don't want to rush into it.	*Seodu reugo sipji anayo.* 서두르고 싶지 않아요.
Take your hands off me.	*Son daeji marayo.* 손 대지 말아요.

Okay, no problem.	*Geuleol kkeyo.* 그럴께요.
Will you spend the night with me?	*Gachi bameul jinael laeyo?* 같이 밤을 지낼래요?
I'd like to go to bed with you.	*Dangsingwa jago sipeoyo.* 당신과 자고 싶어요.
Only if we use a condom.	*Kondomeul sayong handa myeonyo.* 콘돔을 사용한다면요.
We have to be careful about AIDS.	*Ei jeureul josim haeya haeyo.* 에이즈를 조심해야 해요.
That's what they all say.	*Geugeon saram deuli neulsang haneun mari guyo.* 그건 사람들이 늘 상하는 말이구요.
We shouldn't take any risks.	*Wiheomhan geon andwaeyo.* 위험한 건 안돼요.
Do you have a condom?	*Kondom isseoyo?* 콘돔 있어요?
No? Then the answer's no.	*Eopseumyeon andwaeyo.* 없으면 안돼요.

3.9 Congratulations and condolences

Happy birthday.	*Saengil chuka hamnida.* 생일 축하합니다.
Please accept my condolences.	*Aedoreul pyo hamnida.* 애도를 표합니다.
My deepest sympathy.	*Gaseum gipi aedo hamnida.* 가슴 깊이 애도합니다.

3.10 Arrangements

When will I see you again?	*Eonje dasi mannal su innayo?* 언제 다시 만날 수 있나요?
Are you free over the weekend?	*Jumare sigan isseoyo?* 주말에 시간 있어요?

What's the plan, then?	*Museun gyehoegi isseoyo?*
	무슨 계획이 있어요?
Where shall we meet?	*Uri eodiseo mannal kkayo?*
	우리 어디서 만날까요?
Will you pick me/us up?	*Derireo ol geongayo?*
	데리러 올 건가요?
Shall I pick you up?	*Derireo galkkayo?*
	데리러 갈까요?
I have to be home by...	*...kkajineun jibe gaya haeyo*
	...까지는 집에 가야 해요
I don't want to see you anymore.	*Disi mannal saenggak eopseoyo.*
	다시 만날 생각 없어요.
Can I take you home?	*Ji be deryeoda jwodo dwaeyo?*
	집에 데려다 줘도 돼요?

3.11 Being the host(ess)

See also 4 Eating out

Can I offer you a drink?	*Eumnyosu deuril kkayo?*
	음료수 드릴까요?
What would you like to drink?	*Mwo masil laeyo?*
	뭐 마실래요?
Something non-alcoholic, please.	*Alko ol seongbun eomneun geoseuro juseyo.*
	알코올 성분 없는 것으로 주세요.
Would you like a cigarette/cigar?	*Dambae deuril kkayo?*
	담배 드릴까요?
I don't smoke.	*Dambae an piwoyo.*
	담배 안 피워요.
Are you doing anything tonight?	*Oneul bame ha lil isseu seyo?*
	오늘 밤에 할 일 있으세요?
Do you have any plans for today/this afternoon/tonight?	*Oneul/oneul ohu/oneul bame museun gyehoek isseu seyo?*
	오늘/오늘 오후/오늘 밤에 무슨 계획 있으세요?

Can I email/call you?	*Email haedo/jeonhwa haejul laeyo?* 이메일해도/전화해도 돼요?
Will you email/call me?	*Email hae/jeonhwa hae.* 이메일해/전화해.
Can I have your email address/phone number/ Skype address?	*Email/jeonhaw beonho/Skype juso jom gareucheo juseyo?* 이메일/전화번호/스카이프 주소 좀 가르쳐 주세요?
Thanks for everything.	*Yeoreo gagiro goma woyo.* 여러 가지로 고마워요.
It was a lot of fun.	*Jeulgeo wosseoyo.* 즐거웠어요.
Say hello to...	*Insa jeonhae juseyo* ...인사 전해 주세요
All the best.	*Jal jinae seyo.* 잘 지내세요.
Good luck.	*Haeng uneul bi reoyo.* 행운을 빌어요.
When will you be back?	*Eonje dora o seyo?* 언제 돌아오세요?
I'll be waiting for you.	*Gida rigo isseul kkeyo.* 기다리고 있을게요.
I'd like to see you again.	*Tto bwasseu myeon jo ke sseoyo.* 또 봤으면 좋겠어요.
I hope we meet again soon.	*Got dasi bol su isseu myeon jo ke sseoyo.* 곧 다시 볼 수 있으면 좋겠어요.
Here's our address, if you're ever in the United States...	*U ri juso yeyo, miguge omyeon...* 우리 주소예요, 미국에 오면...
You'd be more than welcome.	*Eonjena hwanyeong haeyo.* 언제나 환영해요.

4. Eating out

4.1   At the restaurant
4.2   Ordering
4.3   The bill
4.4   Complaints
4.5   Paying a compliment
4.6   The menu
4.7   Alphabetical list of dishes

4.1 At the restaurant

I'd like to reserve a table for seven o'clock, please.	*Ilgop si e yeyageul hago sipeun deyo.* 일곱 시에 예약을 하고 싶은데요.
A table for two, please.	*Du saram teibeul buta kamnida.* 두 사람 테이블 부탁합니다.
We've reserved.	*Yeyak haesseoyo.* 예약했어요.
We haven't reserved.	*Yeyak an haesseoyo.* 예약 안 했어요.
Is the restaurant open yet?	*Sikdangi imi yeoreon nayo?* 식당이 이미 열었나요?
What time does the restaurant open?	*Myeotsi e yeonayo?* 몇시에 여나요?
What time does the restaurant close?	*Myeotsi e dannayo?* 몇시에 닫나요?
Can we wait for a table?	*Jarireul gida ryeoro doel kkayo?* 자리를 기다려도 될까요?
Do we have to wait long?	*Orae gida reoya hanayo?* 오래 기다려야 하나요?
Is this seat taken?	*I jari e nuga innayo?* 이 자리에 누가 있나요?
Could we sit here/there?	*Yeogi/jeogi anjado doel kkayo?* 여기/저기 앉아도 될까요?

51

Can we sit by the window?	*Changmun jjoge anjado doel kkayo?* 창문 쪽에 앉아도 될까요?
Are there any tables outside?	*Bakka tedo tei beuri innayo?* 바깥에도 테이블이 있나요?
Do you have another chair for us?	*Yeobunui uijaga isseul kkayo?* 여분의 의자가 있을까요?
Do you have a highchair?	*Yu ayong uijaga innayo?* 유아용 의자가 있나요?
Is there a socket for this bottle-warmer?	*Uyu byeong deul sokesi innayo?* 우유병 데울 소켓이 있나요?
Could you warm up this bottle/jar for me?	*I byeongeul jom dewo juseyo?* 이 병을 좀 데워주세요?
Not too hot, please.	*Neomu tteugeopji anke hae juseyo.* 너무 뜨겁지 않게 해 주세요.
Is there somewhere I can change the baby's diaper?	*Gijeogwi gara jul gosi innayo?* 기저귀 갈아 줄 곳이 있나요?
Where are the restrooms?	*Hwajang sireun eodi e isseoyo?* 화장실은 어디에 있어요?

예약 하셨나요?	Do you have a reservation?
성함이 어떻게 되시죠?	What name, please?
이쪽입니다.	This way, please.
이 자리는 예약이 된 자리에요.	This table is reserved.
십 오분 안에 한 자리가 빌 것입니다.	We'll have a table free in fifteen minutes.
기다리시겠습니까?	Would you like to wait?

4.2 Ordering

| We'd like something to eat/drink. | *Mwol jom meogeoss eumyeon/ masyeoss eumyeon jo ke sseoyo.* 뭘 좀 먹었으면/마셨으면 좋겠어요. |
| Could I have a quick meal? | *Ppalli doeneun eumsi geuro juseyo?* 빨리 되는 음식으로 주세요? |

We don't have much time.	*Sigani byeollo eopseoyo.* 시간이 별로 없어요.
We'd like to have a drink first.	*Eumnyosu meonjeo juseyo.* 음료수 먼저 주세요.
Could we see the menu/wine list, please?	*Menyu/podoju mongnogeul jom boyeo juseyo?* 메뉴/포도주목록을 좀 여주시겠어요?
Do you have a menu in English?	*Yeongeoro doen menyu pani innayo?* 영어로 된 메뉴판이 있나요?
Do you have a dish of the day/a tourist menu?	*Oneulrui teukbyeol menyu/yeohaeng jayong menyuga innayo?* 오늘의 특별 메뉴/여행자용 메뉴가 있나요?
We haven't made a choice yet.	*Ajik jeonghaji mot hasseoyo.* 아직 정하지 못했어요.
What do you recommend?	*Eotteon geol chucheonhae usi gesseoyo?* 어떤 걸 추천해 주시겠어요?
What are the local/your specialities?	*I jibangui/i sikdangui teukseon yorineun mwoeyo?* 이 지방의/이 식당의 특선요리는 뭐에요?
I like strawberries/olives.	*Ttalgi/olibeu juseyo.* 딸기/올리브 주세요.
I like meat/fish.	*Gogi reul/saengseoneul byeollo an joa haeyo.* 고기를/생선을 별로 안 좋아해요.
I don't like meat/fish.	*Gogi neun/saengseo neun byeollo an joa haeyo.* 고기는/생선은 별로 안 좋아해요.
What's this?	*Ige mwongayo?* 이게 뭔가요?
Does it have...in it?	*Yeogi e...i deureo innayo?* 여기에...이 들어있나요?
Is it stuffed with...?	*Soge...i deureo innayo?* 속에...이 들어있나요?
What does it taste like?	*Masi eoddaeyo?* 맛이 어때요?

Is this sweet?	*Igeon dangayo?* 이건 단가요?
Is this a hot or a cold dish?	*Igeon ttadeutan yorina chaga un yori ingayo?* 이건 따뜻한 요리나 차가운 요리인가요?
Is this hot/spicy?	*Igeo maewoyo?* 이거 매워요?

무엇을 드시겠습니까?	What would you like?
정하셨어요?	Have you decided?
음료를 먼저 드릴까요?	Would you like a drink first?
어떤 음료를 드릴까요?	What would you like to drink?
...가 모자라요/다 나갔어요	We've run out of...
맛 있게 드세요.	Enjoy your meal/Bon appetit.
더 필요한 것 있으세요?	Is everything all right?
식탁을 치워 드릴까요?	May I clear the table?

Do you have anything else, by any chance?	*Hoksi dareun geosi innayo?* 혹시 다른 것이 있나요?
I'm on a salt-free diet.	*Muyeomsik jung ieyo.* 무염식 중이에요.
I can't eat pork.	*Dwaeji gogireul mot meogeoyo.* 돼지 고기를 못 먹어요.
I can't have sugar.	*Seoltang mot meogeoyo.* 설탕 못 먹어요.
I'm on a fat-free diet.	*Mujibang sigiyo ppeop jung ieyo.* 무지방 식이요법 중이에요.
I can't have spicy food.	*Mae un eum sigeul mot meog eoyo.* 매운 음식을 못 먹어요.
We'll have what those people are having.	*Jeojjok saram deuri meongneun geollo juseyo.* 저쪽 사람들이 먹는 걸로 주세요.
I'd like...	*...juseyo* ...주세요

We're not having...	*...eun an meogeul kkeyo* ...은 안 먹을게요
Could I have some more bread, please?	*Ppang jom deo juseyo?* 빵 좀 더 주세요?
Could I have another bottle of water/ wine, please?	*Mul/wa in han byeong deo juseyo?* 물/와인 한 병 더 주세요?
Could I have another portion of..., please?	*...hana deo chugahae juseyo?* ...하나 더 추가해 주세요?
Could I have the salt and pepper, please?	*Sogeum hago huchu juseyo?* 소금하고 후추 주세요?
Could I have a napkin, please?	*Naepkin jom jusi gesseoyo?* 냅킨 좀 주시겠어요?
Could I have a teaspoon, please?	*Cha sukkarak jom juseyo?* 차 숟가락 좀 주세요?
Could I have an ashtray, please?	*Jaetteori jom juseyo?* 재떨이 좀 주세요?
Could I have some matches, please?	*Seongnyang jom jusi gesseoyo?* 성냥 좀 주시겠어요?
Could I have some toothpicks, please?	*Issu sigae jom jusi gesseoyo?* 이쑤시개 좀 주시겠어요?
Could I have a glass of water, please?	*Mul han jan jusi gesseoyo?* 물 한 잔 주시겠어요?
Could I have a straw please?	*Ppalttae jom juseyo?* 빨대 좀 주세요?
Enjoy your meal/ Bon appetit.	*Mashitge deuseyo.* 맛있게 드세요.
You too!	*Ma sikke deuseyo!* 맛 있게 드세요!
Cheers!	*Geonbae!* 건배!
The next round's on me.	*Daeu meneun jega naelkkeyo.* 다음에는 제가 낼게요.
Could we have a doggy bag, please?	*Nameun geo jom ssa jusi gesseoyo?* 남은 거 좀 싸 주시겠어요?

4.3 The bill

See also 8.2 Settling the bill

How much is this dish?	*Eolma yeyo?* 얼마예요?
Could I have the bill, please?	*Gyesanseo jom juseyo?* 계산서 좀 주세요?
All together.	*Hankkeo beone gyesan halkkeyo.* 한꺼번에 계산 할게요.
Everyone pays separately/ let's go Dutch.	*Gakja ttaro gyesan hapsida.* 각자 따로 계산합시다.
Could we have the menu again, please?	*Menyu paneul dasi gatda juseyo.* 메뉴판을 다시 갖다 주세요.
The…is not on the bill	*…ga gyesa neseo ppajyeo sseoyo* …가 계산에서 빠졌어요

4.4 Complaints

It's taking a very long time.	*Sigani neomu orae geolli neyo.* 시간이 너무 오래 걸리네요.
We've been here an hour already.	*Uriga yeogi han sigani na isseo sseoyo.* 우리가 여기 한 시간이나 있었어요.
This must be a mistake.	*Mwonga jal mot dwaess neyo.* 뭔가 잘 못 됐네요.
This is not what I ordered.	*Igeon jega jumun hange anin deyo.* 이건 제가 주문한게 아닌데요.
I ordered…	*…reul jumunhae sseoyo* …를 주문했어요
There's a dish missing.	*Yori han gajiga ppajeo sseoyo.* 요리 한 가지가 빠졌어요.
This is broken/not clean.	*Igeon buseo jeosseoyo/igeon kkaekkeu taji anayo.* 이건 부서졌어요/이건 깨끗하지 않아요.
The food's cold.	*Eumsigi sigeo sseoyo.* 음식이 식었어요.

The food's not fresh.	*Eumsigi sinseon haji anayo.* 음식이 신선하지 않아요.
The food's too salty/ sweet/spicy.	*I eumsigeun neomu jjayo/neomu darayo/neomu maewoyo.* 이 음식은 너무 짜요/너무 달아요/ 너무 매워요.
The meat's too rare.	*Gogiga neomu deol igeo sseoyo.* 고기가 너무 덜 익었어요.
The meat's overdone.	*Gogireul neomu ikyeon neyo.* 고기를 너무 익혔네요.
The meat's tough.	*Gogiga jilgyeoyo.* 고기가 질겨요.
The meat is off/ has gone bad.	*Gogiga sang haesseoyo.* 고기가 상했어요.
Could I have something else instead of this?	*Igeo daesin dareun geollo juseyo?* 이거 대신 다른 걸로 주세요?
The bill/this amount is not right.	*Gyesani jal mot dwae sseoyo.* 계산이 잘 못 됐어요.
We didn't have this.	*Igeon an meogeon neundeyo.* 이건 안 먹었는데요.
There's no toilet paper in the restroom.	*Hwajang sile hyujiga eopseoyo.* 화장실에 휴지가 없어요.
Will you call the manager, please?	*Jibae ineul bulleo juseyo?* 지배인을 불러주세요?

4.5 Paying a compliment

That was a wonderful meal.	*Masikke jal meogeo sseumnida.* 맛있게 잘 먹었습니다.
The food was excellent.	*Eumsigi neomu masisseo sseoyo.* 음식이 너무 맛있었어요.
The...in particular was delicious.	*Teuki...i masi neyo.* 특히...이 맛있네요.

4.6 The menu

starter/*hors d'oeuvres* **jeonche** 전채	liqueur (after dinner) **julyu** 주류	snacks **seunaeg** 스낵	fish **saengseollyu** 생선류
soups **tangnyu** 탕류	desserts/tea **hu shingnyu/cha** 후식류/차	drinks **eum nyo** 음료	specialties **teugseon yoli** 특선요리
noodles **myeollyu** 면류	main course **mein koseu** 메인 코스	salad **sallade** 살라드	pizza **pija** 피자
meat **yuglyu** 육류	hot pots **jeongollyu** 전골류	pasta **paseuta** 파스타	bread **ppang** 빵
	vegetable dishes **chaesig** 채식	poultry **dalg yoli** 닭요리	

4.7 Alphabetical list of dishes

Korean food is invigorating and varied, with many regions having their own specialities. If you want to taste a variety of dishes in one meal, then try *hanjeongsik* (한정식). This set meal usually consists of two types of soup, ten side dishes, and five types of vegetables and fish.

Bibimbap (비빔밥) is assorted vegetables on steamed rice with red pepper paste sauce.

Bulgogi (불고기) is one of the most popular Korean foods. Thin slices of beef are marinated in soy sauce and sesame oil and cooked on a dome-shaped grill.

Galbi (갈비) or ribs is another very popular Korean food. The ingredients are the same as for *bulgogi*, but cooked over a barbeque grill.

Hamheung naengmyeon (함흥 냉면), a variation of **naengmyeon**, is just noodles and hot pepper paste sauce, without broth.

Kimchi (김치)is an important part of any Korean meal and is made of a spicy mixture of fermented vegetables (most often napa cabbage), chilli, garlic, ginger and other seasonings.

Naengmyeon (냉면), noodles served with cold beef broth, is a favorite summer dish.

Samgyetang (삼계탕) or ginseng chicken soup is another great summer dish in Korea. Especially on Chobok, Jungbok, and Malbok (days that mark the first, middle and last periods of the summer), people eat **samgyetang** to beat the summer heat.

Seolleongtang (설렁탕) is a beef broth soup with chopped scallions. It is served with rice and it goes very well with **kkakttugi**, radish **kimchi**.

Sinseollo (신선로) is a delicious mixture of beef and vegetables cooked in a steamboat pot.

Songpyeon (송편) are small cakes made of rice-flour dough with a filling of sweetened chestnuts and green mung beans. They are a traditional part of Chuseok, the Korean thanksgiving holiday.

5. Getting Around

5.1 Asking directions
5.2 Traffic signs
5.3 The car
5.4 Renting a car
5.5 Breakdowns and repairs
5.6 Motorcycles and bicycles
   The parts of a motorcycle/bicycle
5.7 The gas station
5.8 Hitchhiking

In Korea, cars are driven on the right side of the road and main streets can be very crowded from early morning until late evening. Due to the heavy traffic and often confusing road systems, it may be desirable to hire a driver along with the car, especially in large cities. Travelers who wish to hire a chauffeur-driven car must be prepared to pay the driver's meals and other traveling expenses as well. Bicycle paths are becoming much more common in Korea. Though bikes can be hired in most towns, bikes are not often considered a proper means of transportation on main roads.

Asking directions

Excuse me, could I ask you something?	*Sillye hamnida, mwo jom yeojjwo bolkkeyo?* 실례합니다, 뭐 좀 여쭤 볼게요?
I've lost my way.	*Gireul ireo sseoyo.* 길을 잃었어요.
Is there a …around here?	*I geuncheo e…ga innayo?* 이 근처에…가 있나요?
Is this the way to…?	*Ijjogi…ro ganeun giri mannayo?* 이쪽이…로 가는 길이 맞나요?
Could you tell me how to get to…?	*…ro eotteoke gal su inneunji allyeo juseyo?* …로 어떻게 갈 수 있는지 알려주세요?

How many kilometers is it to…?
…kkaji myeot killo miteo ingayo?
…까지 몇 킬로미터 인가요?

What's the quickest way to…?
…ro ganeunde jeil ppareun giri eodin gayo?
…로 가는데 제일 빠른 길이 어딘가요?

Could you point it out on the map?
Jido eseo eodi inji garikyeo juseyo?
지도에서 어디인지 가리켜 주세요?

여기서 어디로 가야 할 지 잘 모르겠어요.
I don't know my way around here.

길을 잘 못 드셨어요.
You're going the wrong way.

다시… 쪽으로 돌아가야 해요.
You have to go back to…

저기에서부터 표지판을 따라 가세요.
From there on just follow the signs.

저기 가서 다시 물어보세요.
When you get there, ask again.

---

go straight ahead
jigjin
직진

turn right
uho e jeon
우회전

cross
geonneom
건넘

the road/street
gil/lo
길/로

the tunnel
teoneol
터널

the building
geonmul
건물

the river
gang
강

the bridge
gyolyang
교량

at the corner
gilmotung ieseo
길모퉁이에서

turn left
jwa hoejeong
좌회전

follow
ijjog eulo
이쪽으로

the arrow
hwasalpyo
화살표

the grade crossing
gicha geonneolmog
기차 건널목

the 'yield' sign
yangbo
양보

the overpass
goga dolo
고가도로

the intersection/ crossroads
gyo chalo
교차로

the traffic light
sinhodeung
신호등

parking disk (compulsory)
paking diseukeu
파킹 디스크

turn on headlights
teoneol nae jeomdung
터널 내 점등

no access/ no pedestrian access
jeobgeun geumji/ tonghaeng geumji
접근 금지/통행 금지

stop
jeongji
정지

sidewalk
indo/bodo
인도/보도

road assistance (breakdown service)
dolo seubiseu
도로 서비스

service station
chalyang jeongbiso
차량 정비소

Do not obstruct
Banghae haji masio
방해하지 마시오

road closed
dolo pyeswae
도로 폐쇄

curves
keobeu
커브

toll payment
tonghaeng nyo
통행료

impassable shoulder
gasgil sayong geumji
갓길 사용금지

supervised garage/ parking lot
gwanlija sang geun juchajang
관리자 상근 주차장

paying carpark
yulyo juchajang
유료 주차장

parking for a limited period
ilsi jucha
일시 주차

beware, falling rocks
nagseog juui
낙석 주의

no right/left turn
uhoejeon/jwahoejeon geumji
우회전/좌회전 금지

change lanes
chaeson byeon gyeong
차선 변경

train crossing
gicha geonneolmog
기차 건널목

no passing
tonghaeng eumji
통행 금지

maximum headroom
choedae nopi
최대 높이

parking reserved for...
oe jucha geumji
외 주차 금지

detour
uho e
우회

danger(ous)
wiheom
위험

road works
dolo gongsa
도로 공사

road blocked
dolo tongje
도로 통제

right of way
useongwon
우선권

beware
juui/josim
주의/조심

road narrows
job ajim
좁아짐

maximum speed
choedae sogdo
최대 속도

no parking
jucha geumji
주차금지

one way
libang tonghaeng
일방 통행

broken/uneven surface	keep right/left	exit
pason dolo	*ucheug tonghaeng/ jwacheug tonghaeng*	*chulgu*
파손 도로	우측통행/좌측통행	출구

rain or ice for...kms	tow-away area	no entry
ucheonsi...kilo	*gyeon injiyeog*	*jin ib geumji*
우천시...킬로	견인지역	진입 금지

heavy trucks	emergency lane	slow down
daeyong teuleog	*bisangsi chaeon*	*seohaeng*
대형 트럭	비상시 차선	서행

road closed	snow chains required	driveway
dolo kkeut	*seunou chein buchag*	*jin iblo*
도로 끝	스노우 체인 부착	진입로

5.3 The car

(the diagram shows the numbered parts)

	backup light	*baekeop rait*	백업라이트
	fuel pump	*yeollyo peompeu*	연료 펌프
	fan	*pan/hwan punggi*	팬/환풍기
1	battery	*baeteori*	배터리
2	rear light	*mi deung*	미등
3	rear-view mirror	*baek mireo*	백미러
4	gas tank	*yeollyo taenkeu*	연료 탱크
5	spark plugs	*seupakeu peulleogeu*	스파크 플러그
6	side mirror	*saideu mireo*	사이드 미러
7	trunk	*teureongkeu*	트렁크
8	headlight	*haedeu raiteu/jeonjodeung*	해드라이트/전조등
9	air filter	*e eo pilteo*	에어 필터
10	door	*do eo*	도어
11	radiator	*naenggakki*	냉각기
12	brake disc	*beureikeu diseukeu*	브레이크 디스크
13	indicator	*gyegipan*	계기판
14	windshield wiper	*am nyuri waipeo*	앞 유리 와이퍼
15	seat belt	*anjeon belteu*	안전 벨트
16	wheel	*hwil*	휠
17	spare wheel	*seupe bakkwi*	스페어 바퀴

5.4 Renting a car

To rent a car, a driver should have more than one year's experience, an international driver's license, a passport and over 21 years old.

I'd like to rent a…	*…reul billigo sipeun deyo* …를 빌리고 싶은데요
Do I need a (special) license for that?	*Igeol sseuryeo myeon (teuk su) myeonheo jjeungi piryo hangayo?* 이걸 쓰려면 (특수) 면허증이 필요한가요?
I'd like to rent the…for…	*…reul…e sseuryeogo billigo sipeoyo* …를…에 쓰려고 빌리고 싶어요
the…for a day	*…reul haru billigo sipeoyo* …를 하루 빌리고 싶어요
the…for two days	*…reul iteulgan billigo sipeoyo* …를 이틀간 빌리고 싶어요
How much is that per day week?	*Haru e/ilju ire eolma ingayo?* 하루/일주일에 얼마인가요?

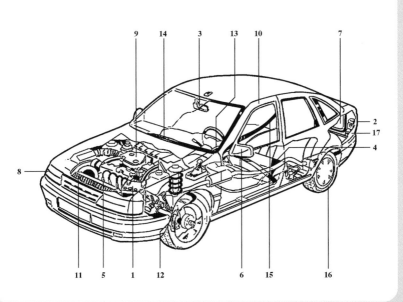

65

How much is the deposit?	*Yechi geumeun eolma ingayo?* 예치금은 얼마인가요?
Could I have a receipt for the deposit?	*Yechigeum yeongsu jeungeul badeul su innayo?* 예치금 영수증을 받을 수 있나요?
How much is the surcharge per kilometer?	*Killo dang chuga yogeumeun eolma ingayo?* 킬로 당 추가 요금은 얼마인가요?
Does that include gas?	*Gireumdo poham hago innayo?* 기름도 포함하고 있나요?
Does that include insurance?	*Boheomdo doenayo?* 보험도 되나요?
What time can I pick the...up?	*...reul myeot si e gajireo omyeon doenayo?* ...를 몇 시에 가지러 오면 되나요?
When does it have to be back (returned)?	*Eonje kkaji bannap haeya hanayo?* 언제까지 반납해야 하나요?
Where's the gas tank?	*Gireum taenkeu neun eodi e innayo?* 기름탱크는 어디에 있나요?
What sort of fuel does it take?	*Eotteon yeollyoreul sseunayo?* 어떤 연료를 쓰나요?

5.5 Breakdowns and repairs

My car has broken down, could you help me?	*Gojangi nanneunde, jom dowa juseyo?* 고장이 났는데, 좀 도와주세요?
I've run out of gas.	*Gireumi da tteoreojeo gayo.* 기름이 다 떨어져가요.
I've locked the keys in the car.	*Yeolsoeleul dugo cha meuneul jamga sseoyo.* 열쇠를 두고 차 문을 잠갔어요.
The car/motorbike/ moped won't start.	*Cha/otobai/moteu jajeon geoga chulbari an dweyo.* 차/오토바이/모터 자전거가 출발이 안 돼요.
Could you call a garage for me, please?	*Ka ssenteo e jeonhwa jom hae juseyo?* 카 센터에 전화 좀 해 주세요?

Could you call the breakdown service for me, please?	*Suri seobi seu e yeollak jom hae juseyo?* 수리서비스에 연락 좀 해 주세요?
Could you give me a lift to the nearest garage?	*Gakka un jeongbiso kkaji jom deryeoda juseyo?* 가까운 정비소까지 좀 데려다 주세요?
Could you give me a lift to the nearest town?	*Gakka un sinae kkaji jom deryeoda juseyo?* 가까운 시내까지 좀 데려다 주세요?
Could you give me a lift to the nearest telephone booth?	*Gakka un jeonhwa bakseu kkaji jom deryeoda juseyo?* 가까운 전화박스까지 좀 데려다 주세요?
Could you give me the nearest emergency phone?	*Gakka un gingeup jeonhwagi inneun gose jom deryeoda juseyo?* 가까운 긴급 전화기 있는 곳에 좀 데려다 주세요?
Can we take my moped?	*Je moteu jajeon georeul gajigo gado dwaeyo?* 제 모터 자전거를 가지고 가도 돼요?
Could you tow me to a garage?	*Jeongbiso kkaji gyeoninhae juseyo?* 정비소까지 견인해 주세요?
There's probably something wrong with... (See pages 65 and 69)	*...e munjega inneun geot gatayo* ...에 문제가 있는 것 같아요
Can you fix it?	*Gochil su innayo?* 고칠 수 있나요?
Could you fix my tire?	*Taieo reul go chyeo juseyo?* 타이어를 좀 고쳐 주세요?
Could you change this wheel?	*I bakwireul bakkwo juseyo?* 이 바퀴를 바꿔 주세요?
Can you fix it so it'll get me to...?	*...kkaji gal su ittorok gochil su isseoyo?* ...까지 갈 수 있도록 고칠 수 있어요?
Which garage can help me?	*Eoddeon jeongbi soro gamyeon doenayo?* 어떤 정비소로 가면 되나요?
When will my car/ bicycle be ready?	*Cha/jajeongeo suriga eonje kkaji doel kkayo?* 차/자전거 수리가 언제까지 될까요?

Have you finished yet?	*Beolsseo kkeunnae syeo sseoyo?* 벌써 끝내셨어요?
Can I wait for it here?	*Yeogiseo gida ryeodo doeyo?* 여기서 기다려도 될까요?
How much will it cost?	*Eolma jeongdoga deul kkayo?* 얼마 정도가 들까요?
Could you itemize the bill?	*Cheonggu seo e hangmok byeollo sseo juseyo?* 청구서에 항목별로 써 주세요?
Could you give me a receipt for insurance purposes?	*Boheom cheori hal yeongsu jeungeul juseyo?* 보험 처리 할 영수증을 주세요?

5.6 Motorcycles and bicycles

See the diagram on page 69

Bicycle paths are common in towns and cities and their use is strongly recommended. Bikes can usually be rented at tourist centers. The maximum speed for mopeds is 40 km/h both inside and outside town centers. Crash helmets are compulsory.

손님 차/자전거 부품이 없습니다.	I don't have parts for your car/bicycle.
다른 곳에서 부품을 가져 와야 해요.	I have to get the parts from somewhere else.
부품을 주문해야 해요.	I have to order the parts.
반나절 걸릴 거에요.	That'll take half a day.
하루 정도 걸릴 거에요.	That'll take a day.
며칠 걸릴 거에요.	That'll take a few days.
일주일 걸릴 거에요.	That'll take a week.
차가 완전히 망가졌네요.	Your car is a write-off.
고칠 수 없어요.	It can't be repaired.
차/오토바이/모터 자전거/ 자전거를... 시에 찾으러 오세요.	The car/motorcycle/moped/ bicycle will be ready at ...o'clock.

The parts of a motorcycle/bicycle

(the diagram shows the numbered parts*)

1	rear wheel	*dwit bakwi*	뒷 바퀴
2	gear change	*gieo*	기어
3	chain	*chein*	체인
4	headlight	*jeonjodeung*	전조등
5	pump	*peompeu*	펌프
6	reflector	*bansa gyeong*	반사경
7	brake shoe	*breikeu*	브레이크
8	brake cable	*breikeu keibeul*	브레이크 케이블
9	carrier straps	*sopum geoli*	소품걸이
10	spoke	*seupokeu*	스포크
11	mudguard	*jinheuk baji*	진흙받이
12	handlebar	*sonjabi*	손잡이
13	toe clip	*bal gojeoonggi*	발 고정기
14	drum brake	*deureom beure ikeu*	드럼 브레이크
15	valve	*baelbeu*	밸브
16	valve tube	*baelbeu gwan*	밸브 관
17	gear cable	*gieo keibeul*	기어 케이블
18	front wheel	*ap bakwi*	앞 바퀴
19	seat	*uija*	의자

*Most parts are loanwords from English.

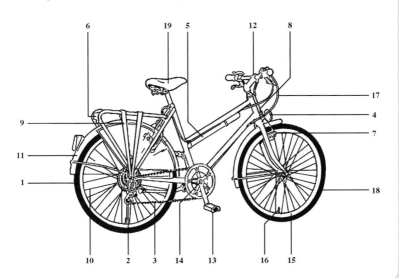

How many kilometers to the next gas station, please?	*Daeum juyuso kkajineun myeot killo ingayo?* 다음 주유소까지는 몇 킬로인가요?
I would like...liters of	*...riteo neoeo juseyo* …리터 넣어주세요
– super	*supeo* 수퍼
– leaded	*yuyeon* 유연
– unleaded	*muyeon* 무연
– diesel	*dijel* 디젤
…worth of gas	*...riteo eochi* …리터 어치
Fill her up, please.	*Gadeuk chaewo juseyo.* 가득 채워 주세요.
Could you check the oil level, please?	*Oileul jeomgeomhae juseyo?* 오일을 점검해 주세요?
Could you check the tire pressure, please?	*Taieo amnyeogeul jeomgeomhae juseyo?* 타이어 압력을 점검해 주세요?
Could you change the oil, please?	*Oileul bakkwo juseyo?* 오일을 바꿔주세요?
Could you clean the windshield, please?	*Am nyurireul dakka juseyo?* 앞 유리를 닦아 주세요?
Could you wash the car, please?	*Secha hae juseyo?* 세차 해 주세요?

5.8 Hitchhiking

Hitchhiking is very rare in Korea. Getting a ride from a stranger may be difficult, but these are some common directions and courtesies. It's generally easier to get a lift if you are rather well-dressed and clean shaven. Try motorway service stations for the best chances of hitching a ride. These also offer free roadmaps, Internet access and excellent cheap food.

Where are you heading?
Eodi gayo?
어디 가요?

Can you give me a lift?
Taewo jusi gesseoyo?
태워 주시겠어요?

Can my friend come too?
Je chingudo tado deyo?
제 친구도 타도 돼요?

I'd like to go to...
...e gago sipeun deyo
...에 가고 싶은데요

Is that on the way to...?
...ro ganeun giri seyo?
...로 가는 길이세요?

Could you drop me off...?
...e jom naeryeo juseyo?
...에 좀 내려 주세요?

Could you drop me
off here?
Yeogiseo jom naeryeo juseyo?
여기서 좀 내려주세요?

Could you drop me off
at the entrance to
the highway?
*Gosok doro jinnip hal ttae jom
naeryeo juseyo?*
고속도로 진입할 때 좀 내려주세요?

Could you drop me off
in the center?
Senteo e jom naeryeo juseyo?
센터에 좀 내려주세요?

Could you drop me off at
the next intersection?
Daeum gyocharo eseo jom sewo juseyo?
다음 교차로에서 좀 세워 주세요?

Could you stop
here, please?
Yeogi e jom sewo juseyo?
여기에 좀 세워 주세요?

I'd like to get out here.
Yeogi e naeryeo juseyo.
여기서 내려 주세요.

Thanks for the lift.
Taewo jusyeoseo gamsa hamnida.
태워 주셔서 감사합니다.

6. Arrival and Departure

6.1 General
6.2 Customs
6.3 Luggage
6.4 Questions to Passengers
6.5 Tickets
6.6 Information
6.7 Airplanes
6.8 Trains
6.9 Taxis

There are about eighteen subway lines in Seoul (with more coming up in the next few years), each indicated by a different color. They link the farthest parts of Seoul and its satellite cities. Transfers between lines may be made at various stations. Trains operate at intervals of 2.5 to 3 minutes during the morning and evening rush hours, and at intervals of 4 to 6 minutes the rest of the day.

There are three kinds of urban buses running in Seoul: City, City Express and Deluxe Express. The City Express buses (*jwaseok*) are more comfortable than City buses (*ilban*). There is another type of bus (*maeul*) that covers residential areas without convenient transportation such as the subway or regular buses. Usually these buses are smaller and cheaper than the normal buses. Fares have to be paid in cash.

Ask your hotel front desk or the Bus Route Information Center where the bus stops are and which number to take.

 General

(...시)...행 기차가...분까지(정도) 연착되고 있습니다	The [time] train to...has been delayed by (about)...minutes
지금...행 기차가 승강장에 도착하고 있습니다	The train to...is now arriving

...발 기차가 승강장에 들어오고
있습니다
다음 역은 ... 입니다.

The train from...is
now arriving
The next station is...

Where does this train go to?	*I gichaneun eodiro ganayo?* 이 기차는 어디로 가나요?
Does this boat go to...?	*I baeneun ...ro ganayo?* 이 배는 ...로 가나요?
Can I take this bus to...?	*...ro garyeomyeon i beoseureul tamyeon doenayo?* ...로 가려면 이 버스를 타면 되나요?
Does this train stop at...?	*I gichaga ...e seonayo?* 이 기차가 ...에 서나요?
Is this seat taken/ free/reserved?	*I jari e nuga isseum nikka/binjari imnikka/yeoyak doen jari ingayo?* 이 자리에 누가 있습니까/빈자리 입니까/예약된 자리인가요?
I've reserved...	*...reul yeyak haenneun deoyo* ...를 예약했는데요
Could you tell me where I have to get off for...?	*...ro garyeo myeon eodi eseo naeri myeon doenayo?* ...로 가려면 어디에서 내리면 되나요?
Could you let me know when we get to...?	*...e dochak hamyeon allyeo juseyo?* ...에 도착하면 알려 주세요?
Where are we?	*Yeogiga eodin gayo?* 여기가 어딘가요?
Do I have to get off here?	*Yeogi eseo naeryeoya hanayo?* 여기에서 내려야 하나요?
Have we already passed...?	*Beolsseo ...reul jina chyeo sseoyo?* 벌써...를 지나쳤어요?
How long have I been asleep?	*Jega jameul eolmana jannayo?* 제가 잠을 얼마나 잤나요?
How long does the train stop here?	*Gichaga yeogi e eolma ttongan meomchul kkayo?* 기차가 여기에 얼마동안 멈출까요?

Can I come back on the same ticket?	*Doragal ttae gateun pyoreul sseumyeon doenayo?* 돌아갈 때 같은 표를 쓰면 되나요?
How long is this ticket valid for?	*I pyoneun yuhyo gigani eolma dongan ingayo?* 이 표는 유효기간이 얼마동안 인가요?
How much is the extra fare for the high speed train?	*Gosongyeol chareul taryeo myeon chuga biyongi eolma ingayo?* 고속열차를 타려면 추가 비용이 얼마인가요?

6.2 Customs

여권 주세요.	Your passport, please.
영주권 보여 주세요.	Your green card, please.
자동차 등록서류 주세요.	Your vehicle documents, please.
사증/비자 보여주세요.	Your visa, please.
어디로 가나요?	Where are you going?
얼마동안 머물 계획인가요?	How long are you planning to stay?
신고할 것이 있습니까?.	Do you have anything to declare?
이것 열어주세요.	Open this, please.

My children are entered on this passport.	*Uri ai deureun i yeokkwo neuro deureo wasseoyo.* 우리 아이들은 이 여권으로 들어왔어요.
I'm traveling through…	*…ro yeohaenghal geoyeyo* …로 여행할 거에요
I'm going on vacation to…	*…ro huga galgeo yeyo* …로 휴가 갈 거에요
I'm on a business trip.	*Chuljjang jung ieyo.* 출장 중이에요.
I don't know how long I'll be staying.	*Eolmana meomu reuljji ajik moreu gesseoyo.* 얼마나 머무를지 아직 모르겠어요.
I'll be staying here a week.	*Yeogi e iluil meomul geoeyo.* 여기 일주일 머물 거에요.

I'll be staying here for a weekend/a few days.	*Yeogi e jumal/myeochil dongan meomul geoeyo.*
	여기에 주말/며칠동안 머물 거에요.
I'll be staying here for two weeks.	*Yeogi e ijuil meomul geoeyo.*
	여기 이주일 머물 거에요.
I've got nothing to declare.	*Singohal geosi eopsseoyo.*
	신고할 것이 없어요.
I have...	*...ga isseoyo*
	...가 있어요
a carton of cigarettes	*dambae han boru*
	담배 한 보루
a bottle of...	*...han byeong*
	...한 병
some souvenirs	*ginyeompum*
	기념품
These are personal items.	*Igeon gaein mulgeo nieyo.*
	이건 개인 물건이에요.
These are not new.	*Igeon saegeosi ani eyo.*
	이건 새 것이 아니에요.
Here's the receipt.	*Yeongsujeung yeogi isseoyo.*
	영수증 여기 있어요.
This is for private use.	*Igeon gaein yongdoro sangeo eyo.*
	이건 개인 용도로 산 거에요.
How much import duty do I have to pay?	*Suip gwansereul eolmana naeya hanayo?*
	수입관세를 얼마나 내야 하나요?
May I go now?	*Ije gado doenayo?*
	이제 가도 되나요?

6.3 Luggage

Porter!	*Yeogiyo!*
	여기요!
Could you take my luggage to...?	*I jimeul...ro omgyeo juseyo?*
	이 짐을...로 옮겨주세요?
How much do I owe you?	*Eolmareul deuri meun doenayo?*
	얼마를 드리면 되나요?

| Where can I find a cart? | *Kateuneun eodi e innayo?* |
| | 카트는 어디에 있나요? |

| Could you store this luggage for me? | *I jimeul jom bogwanhae juseyo?* |
| | 이 짐을 좀 보관해 주세요? |

| Where are the luggage lockers? | *Mulpum bogwan soneun eodi e innayo?* |
| | 물품 보관소는 어디에 있나요? |

| I can't get the locker open. | *Bogwan hameul yeol suga eopseoyo.* |
| | 보관함을 열 수가 없어요. |

| How much is it per item per day? | *Haru e han pummok dang eolma ingayo?* |
| | 하루에 한 품목 당 얼마인가요? |

| This is not my bag/suitcase. | *Igeon je gabang/jim anin deyo.* |
| | 이건 제 가방/짐 아닌데요. |

| There's one item/bag/ suitcase missing. | *Han gae/gabang/jim eopseo jyeo sseoyo.* |
| | 한 개/가방/짐 없어졌어요. |

| My suitcase is damaged. | *Je jim e sonsangi saenggyeo sseoyo.* |
| | 제 짐 제 손상이 생겼어요. |

| My luggage has not arrived. | *Je jimeun ajik an wasseoyo.* |
| | 제 짐은 아직 안 왔어요. |

| Will I be compensated for the delayed/lost luggage? | *Jiyeon dwoen/naoji anneun jimeul daehan bosangi innayo?* |
| | 지연된/나오지 않는 짐에 대한 보상이 있나요? |

| Can you please send my luggage to this address? | *Je jimeun i juso e boneju shipshio?* |
| | 제 짐은 이 주소에 보내주십시오? |

| The lock has been broken. | *Jamulsoe neun busweo jyeosseoyo.* |
| | 자물쇠는 부숴졌어요. |

| Where is the luggage forwarding service? | *Suryeongji jeonsong seobi seuneun eodi yeyo?* |
| | 수령지 전송 서비스는 어디예요? |

6.4 Questions to passengers

Destination

| 어디로 가나요? | Where are you traveling to? |
| 언제 떠나요? | When are you leaving? |

...는...시에 출발합니다	Your...leaves at...
...를 바꿔야 해요	You have to change at...
...에서 내려야 해요	You have to get off at...
...를 통해서/경유해서 가야 해요	You have to go via....
...(일)에 출발해요	The outward journey is on...
...(일)에 도착해요	The return journey is on...

...시까지는 타야/탑승해야
  합니다
	You have to be on board
	  by....(o'clock)

Inside the vehicle

표 주세요.	Tickets, please.
예약(표) 주세요.	Your reservation, please.
여권 주세요.	Your passport, please.
다른 자리에 앉으셨어요.	You're in the wrong seat.

뭔가 실수를 한 것 같은데요/...
  를 잘 못 한 것 같은데요
	You have made a mistake/
	  You are in the wrong...

여기는 예약이 된 자리예요.	This seat is reserved.
추가 비용을 내야 해요.	You'll have to pay extra.
...가...분 연착되고 있습니다	The...has been delayed by... minutes

6.5 Tickets

Where can I...?	*...neun eodi eseo hamyeon doenayo?* ...는 어디에서 하면 되나요?
– buy a ticket?	*Pyoneun eodi eseo parayo?* 표는 어디에서 팔아요?
– reserve a seat?	*Jwaseogeun eodi eseo* *yeyak hamyeon doenayo?* 좌석은 어디에서 예약하면 되나요?
– reserve a flight?	*Bihaenggi pyoneun eodi eseo* *yeyak hamyeon doenayo?* 비행기 표는 어디에서 예약하면 되나요?

Could I have…for…please?	***…haeng …reul juseyo?***
	…행…를 주세요?
A single to…please	***…haeng pyeondo hanjang juseyo***
	…행 편도 한 장 주세요
A return ticket, please.	***Wangbok han jang juseyo.***
	왕복 한 장 주세요.
first class	***iltteung seok***
	일등석
second class	***ideung seok***
	이등석
economy class	***ilban seok***
	일반석
I'd like to reserve a seat/ berth/cabin.	***Jwaseok/chimdae/seonsil reul yeyak hago sipeun deyo.***
	좌석/침대/선실을 예약하고 싶은데요.
I'd like to reserve an aisle seat.	***Tongno jjok jwaseokeul yeyak hago shipeun deyo.***
	통로 쪽 좌석을 예약하고 싶은데요.
I'd like to reserve a top/ middle/bottom berth in the sleeping car.	***Chimdaecha wi/gaunde/arae chimdaereul yeyak hago sipeun deyo.***
	침대차 위/가운데/아래 침대를 예약하고 싶은데요.
smoking/non-smoking	***heubyeon/geumyeon***
	흡연/금연
by the window	***changga jjok***
	창가 쪽
single/double	***irinseok/i inseok***
	일인석/이인석
at the front/back	***apjjok/dwijjok***
	앞쪽/뒤쪽
There are…of us	***…myeong isseoyo***
	…명 있어요
We have a car/trailer.	***Chaga/teureil ieoga isseoyo.***
	차가/트레일러가 있어요.
We have…bicycles.	***Jajeongeo…daereul gajigo isseoyo.***
	자전거…대를 가지고 있어요.
Do you have a…?	***…ga innayo?***
	…가 있나요?

weekly travel card	*ju jeonggikkwon isseoyo* 주 정기권 있어요
monthly season ticket	*wol jeonggikkwon isseoyo* 월 정기권 있어요
Where's…?	*…neun eodi innayo?* …는 어디 있나요?
Where's the information desk?	*Annae soneun eodi e innayo?* 안내소는 어디에 있나요?

6.6 Information

Where can I find a schedule?	*Unhaeng siganpyo neun eodi innayo?* 운행시간표는 어디 있나요?
Where's the…desk?	*…soneun eodi innayo?* …소는 어디 있나요?
Do you have a map with the bus/subway routes?	*Beoseu/jihacheol noseon jidoga innayo?* 버스/지하철 노선 지도가 있나요?
Do you have a schedule?	*Unhaeng siganpyo gajigo innayo?* 운행시간표 가지고 있나요?
Will I get my money back?	*Hwanbul hae junayo?* 환불해 주나요?
I'd like to go to…	*…e gago sipeun deyo* …에 가고 싶은데요
I'd like to confirm/cancel/ change my reservation for/trip to…	*…haeng yeyageul hwagin/chwiso/ byeongyeong hago sipeun deyo* …행 예약을 확인/취소/변경하고 싶은데요
What is the quickest way to get there?	*Geogi kkaji ganeun jeil ppareun giri eodin gayo?* 거기까지 가는 제일 빠른 길이 어딘가요?
How much is a single/ return to…?	*…haeng pyeondo/wangbokpyo gapseun eolma yeyo?* …행 편도/왕복표 값은 얼마예요?
Do I have to pay extra?	*Chuga biyongeul naeya hanayo?* 추가 비용을 내야 하나요?

Can I break my journey with this ticket?	*I pyoro junggane naeryeotda dasi tal su isseoyo?* 이 표로 중간에 내렸다 다시 탈 수 있어요?
How much luggage am I allowed?	*Jimeun eolma kkaji dwaeyo?* 짐은 얼마까지 돼요?
Is this a direct train?	*Igeon jikhaeng ingayo?* 이건 직행인가요?
Do I have to change?	*Gara taya dwaeyo?* 갈아 타야 돼요?
Does the plane stop anywhere?	*Bihaeng giga eodi e deulleu nayo?* 비행기가 어디에 들르나요?
Will there be any stopovers?	*Eodi gyeongyu haeseo gayo?* 어디 경유해서 가요?
Does the boat stop at any other ports on the way?	*I baeneun gadaga eodi deulleoyo?* 이 배는 가다가 어디 들러요?
Does the train/bus stop at…?	*I gicha/beoseuga …e seoyo?* 이 기차/버스가…에 서요?
Where do I get off?	*Eodiseo naeryeoyo?* 어디서 내려요?
Is there a connection to…?	*…ro ganeun yeongye pyeoni innayo?* …로 가는 연결편이 있나요?
How long do I have to wait?	*Eolmana gida ryeoya haeyo?* 얼마나 기다려야 해요?
When does…leave?	*…ga eonje tteonayo?* …가 언제 떠나요?
What time does the first/next/last…leave?	*Cheot/daeum/majimak …neun myeot si e tteonayo?* 첫/다음/마지막…는 몇 시에 떠나요?
How long does…take?	*…neun eolmana geolli nayo?* …는 얼마나 걸리나요?
What time does it arrive in…?	*…e myeot si e dochak haeyo?* …에 몇 시에 도착해요?
Where does the…to…leave from?	*…haeng…ga eodiseo chulbar haeyo?* …행…가 어디서 출발해요?
Is this the train/bus…to…?	*…ro ganeun gicha/beoseu innayo?* …로 가는 기차/버스 있나요?

6.7 Airplanes

On arrival at one of Korea's many international and domestic airports, you will find the following signs:

check-in *chekeu in* 체크 인	international *gugjeseon* 국제선	domestic flights *gugnaeseon* 국내선
arrivals *dochag* 도착	departures *chulbal* 출발	

6.8 Trains

Korea is well-served by an extensive network of express and local trains operated by the Korean National Railroad. Special package tours are available for foreign travelers who can choose first class, standard class and sleeping cars.

6.9 Taxis

for hire *imdae* 임대	not occupied *bin cha* 빈 차	taxi stand *taegsi seungchajang* 택시 승차장

Taxi!	*Taeksi!* 택시!
Could you get me a taxi, please?	*Taeksi jom bulleo juseyo?* 택시 좀 불러 주세요?
Could you turn on the meter, please?	*Miteogi ollyeo juseyo?* 미터기 올려 주세요?
Where can I find a taxi around here?	*I geuncheo eodi eseo taeksireul jabeul su innayo?* 이 근처 어디에서 택시를 잡을 수 있나요?
Could you take me to..., please?	*...kkaji deryeo da juseyo?* ...까지 데려다 주세요?

to this address	*kkaji gamnida* 까지 갑니다
to the…hotel	*…hotel kkaji gayo* …호텔까지 가요
to the town/city center	*sinae e ga juseyo* 시내에 가 주세요
to the station	*yeoge gamnida* 역에 갑니다
to the airport, please	*gonghange gayo* 공항에 가요
How much is the trip to…?	*…kkaji eolma yeyo?* …까지 얼마예요?
How far is it to…?	*…kkaji eolmana meongayo?* …까지 얼마나 먼가요?
I'm in a hurry.	*Jom geup haeyo.* 좀 급해요.
Could you speed up/ slow down a little?	*Jom deo ppalli/cheoncheonhi ga juseyo?* 좀 더 빨리/천천히 가 주세요?
Could you take a different route?	*Dareun gillo gajuseyo?* 다른 길로 가 주세요?
I'd like to get out here, please.	*Yeogi sewo juseyo.* 여기 세워 주세요.
Go…	*…gapsida* …갑시다
You have to go…here.	*Yeogiseo…gaya haeyo.* 여기서…가야 해요.
Go straight ahead.	*Apeuro ddokbaro gaseyo.* 앞으로 똑바로 가세요.
Turn left/Turn right.	*Jwahwoe jeo ieyo/Uheo jeo ieyo.* 좌회전이에요/우회전에요.
This is it/We're here.	*Da wasseoyo.* 다 왔어요.
Could you wait a minute for me, please?	*Jamsiman gidaryeo juseyo?* 잠시만 기다려 주세요?

7. A Place to Stay

7.1 General
7.2 Hotels/B&Bs/apartments/
    holiday rentals
7.3 Complaints
7.4 Departure
7.5 Camping/backpacking
    Camping equipment

7.1 General

얼마나 오래 계실 건가요?	How long will you be staying?
이 용지를 작성해 주세요.	Fill out this form, please.
여권 좀 보여주세요?	Could I see your passport?
예치금이 필요해요.	I'll need a deposit.
선불로/미리 지불해야만 합니다.	You'll have to pay in advance.

My name is...
Je ireu meun...imnida
제 이름은... 입니다

I've made a reservation.
Yeyageul haesseoyo.
예약을 했어요.

How much is it per
night/week/month?
*Harutbam/han ju/han dare
eolma ingayo?*
하룻밤/한 주/한 달에 얼마인가요?

We'll be staying at
least...nights/weeks.
Yeogi e jeogeodo...il/ju meomul kkeo eyo.
여기에 적어도...일/주 머물 거에요.

We don't know yet.
Ajik jal moreu gesseoyo.
아직 잘 모르겠어요.

Do you allow pets?
Aewan dongmuldo heoyong doenayo?
애완동물도 허용되나요?

Could you get me a
taxi, please?
Taeksireul bulleo juseyo?
택시를 불러 주세요?

What time does the door open/close?	*Myeotsi e muneul yeoseyo/dadeu seyo?*
	몇 시에 문을 여세요/닫으세요?
Is there any mail for me?	*Jeohante on upyeonmul innayo?*
	저한테 온 우편물 있나요?

7.2 Hotels/B&Bs/apartments/holiday rentals

Do you have a single/ double room available?	*Irinyong/iinyong binbang innayo?*
	일인용/이인용 빈 방 있나요?
per person/per room	*irindang/bang hanadang*
	일인당/방 하나 당
Does that include breakfast/lunch/dinner?	*Achim/jeomsim/jeonyeok siksado poham doenayo?*
	아침/점심/저녁 식사도 포함되나요?
Could we have two adjoining rooms?	*Buteo inneun bangeuro dugae juseyo?*
	붙어 있는 방으로 두 개 주세요?
with/without toilet/ bath/shower	*hwajangsil/yoksil/syawo siri inneun/ eomneun*
	화장실/욕실/샤워실이 있는/없는
facing the street	*giljjo geuro hyanghaneun*
	길쪽으로 향하는
at the back	*dwijjoge*
	뒤쪽에
with/without sea view	*bada gyeongchiga bo ineun/bo iji anneun*
	바다 경치가 보이는/보이지 않는
Is there...in the hotel?	*Hotere ...ga innayo?*
	호텔에...가 있나요?
Is there an elevator in the hotel?	*Hotere seung ganggi/elli beiteoga innayo?*
	호텔에 승강기/엘리베이터가 있나요?
Do you have room service?	*Rum seobiseu doenayo?*
	룸서비스 되나요?
Could I see the room?	*Bangeul bolsu isseul kkayo?*
	방을 볼 수 있을까요?
I'll take this room.	*I bangeuro halkkeyo.*
	이 방으로 할게요.
We don't like this one.	*Igeon ma eume deulji anneyo.*
	이건 마음에 들지 않네요.

Do you have a larger/ less expensive room?	*Jom deo bissan/ssan bangi innayo?* 좀 더 비싼/싼 방이 있나요?
What time's breakfast?	*Achim siksaneun myeotsi ingayo?* 아침 식사는 몇 시 인가요?
Where's the dining room?	*Sikdangeun eodi e innayo?* 식당은 어디에 있나요?
Can I have breakfast in my room?	*Je bangeseo achimeul meogeodo doenayo?* 제 방에서 아침을 먹어도 되나요?
Where's the emergency exit/fire escape?	*Bisang guneun/hwajae daepi guneun eodi ingayo?* 비상구는/화재 대피구는 어디인가요?
Where can I park my car safely?	*Chaneun eodi e jucha hamyeon doenayo?* 차는 어디에 주차하면 되나요?
The key to room…, please.	*…hosil yeolsoe juseyo.* …호실 열쇠 주세요.
Could you put this in the safe, please?	*Igeol bogwanhae juseyo?* 이걸 보관해 주세요?
Could you wake me at…tomorrow?	*Naeil …si e kkaewo juseyo?* 내일…시에 깨워 주세요?
Could you find a babysitter for me?	*A i bwa jul saramrul chajabwa juseyo?* 아이 봐 줄 사람을 찾아봐 주세요?
Could I have an extra blanket?	*Yeobunui damyoga piryo haeyo?* 여분의 담요가 필요해요?
What days do the cleaners come in?	*Cheongso hareo museun yoire onayo?* 청소하러 무슨 요일에 오나요?
When are the sheets/ towels dish towels changed?	*Siteu/sugeon/haengjuneun eonje gara junayo?* 시트/수건/행주는 언제 갈아주나요?

A Place to Stay

7

화장실과 샤워실은 같은 층에/ 실내에 있습니다.	The toilet and shower are on the same floor/in the room.
이쪽으로 오세요.	This way please.
손님의 방은…층, …호실입니다	Your room is on the… floor, number…

Complaints

We can't sleep because it's too noisy.	*Sikkeureo woseo jameul jalsuga eopseoyo.* 시끄러워서 잠을 잘 수가 없어요.
Could you turn the radio down, please?	*Radio sorireul jom nachwo juseyo?* 라디오 소리를 좀 낮춰 주세요?
We're out of toilet paper.	*Hwajangsil hyujireul da sseoss eoyo.* 화장실 휴지를 다 썼어요.
There aren't any.../ there's not enough...	*...ga eopseoyo/moja rayo* ...가 없어요/모자라요
The bed linen's dirty.	*Chimdae yoga jijeobun haeyo.* 침대 요가 지저분해요.
The room hasn't been cleaned.	*Bangi kkaekkeut hajiga anayo.* 방이 깨끗하지가 않아요.
The kitchen is not clean.	*Bueogi kkaekkeut haji anayo.* 부엌이 깨끗하지 않아요.
The kitchen utensils are dirty.	*Bueok yongguga jijeobun haeyo.* 부엌 용구가 지저분해요.
The heating isn't working.	*Na bangi andoeyo.* 난방이 안 되요.
There's no (hot) water/electricity.	*(Tteugeoun) muri an nawayo/ jeongiga an deureo wayo.* (뜨거운) 물이 안 나와요/전기가 안 들어와요.
...doesn't work/is broken	*...ga andoeyo/gojang nasseoyo* ...가 안 되요/고장 났어요
Could you have that fixed, please?	*Igeot son bwa juseyo?* 이것 손 봐주세요?
Could I have another room/site?	*Dareun bang/goseul juseyo?* 다른 방/곳을 주세요?
The bed creaks terribly.	*Chimdaega simhage ppigeok georyeoyo.* 침대가 심하게 삐걱거려요.
The bed sags.	*Chimdaega naryeo anjayo.* 침대가 내려 앉아요.

Could I have a board under the mattress?	*Maeteu riseu mite paneul dae juseyo?* 매트리스 밑에 판을 대 주세요?
It's too noisy.	*Neomu sikkeureo woyo.* 너무 시끄러워요.
There are a lot of insects/bugs.	*Beollaega neomu manayo.* 벌레가 너무 많아요.
This place is full of mosquitoes.	*Yeogin mogiga neomu manayo.* 여긴 모기가 너무 많아요.
This place is full of cockroaches.	*Yeogin bakwi beollaega neomu manayo.* 여긴 바퀴벌레가 너무 많아요.

7.4 Departure

See also 8.2 Settling the bill

I'm leaving tomorrow.	*Naeil tteonal yejeongi eyo.* 내일 떠날 예정이에요.
Could I pay my bill please?	*Yogeum gyesan hago sipeun deyo?* 요금 계산하고 싶은데요?
What time should we check out?	*Myeotsi e chekeu aut hamyeon doenayo?* 몇 시에 체크아웃 하면 되나요?
Could I have my deposit/passport back, please?	*Yechigeum/yeokkwoneul dollyeo juseyo?* 예치금/여권을 돌려 주세요?
We're in a big hurry.	*Jigeum neomu geup haeyo.* 지금 너무 급해요.
Could we leave our luggage here until we leave?	*Tteonal ddaekkaji jimeul yeogi dwodo doenayo?* 떠날 때까지 짐을 여기 둬도 되나요?
Thanks for your hospitality.	*Chinjeol hage daehae jusyeoseo gamsa hamnida.* 친절하게 대해 주셔서 감사합니다.

7.5 Camping/backpacking

See the diagram below

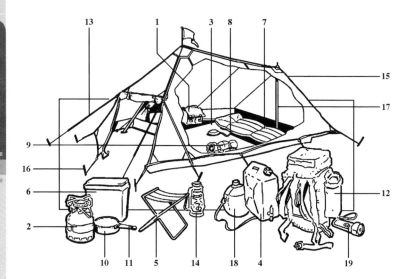

야영지를 직접 고를 수 있어요.	You can pick your own site.
야영지를 배정할 거예요.	You'll be allocated a site.
이게 야영지 번호 입니다.	This is your site number.
이것을 손님 차에 단단히 붙여 주세요.	Please stick this firmly to your car.
이 카드를 잃어버리면 안 됩니다.	You must not lose this card.

Where's the manager?	*Maenijeoneon eodi e innayo?* 매니저는 어디에 있나요?
Are we allowed to camp here?	*Yeogi e yayeong haedo doenayo?* 여기에 야영해도 되나요?
There are...of us and we have...tents.	*...myeonggwa tenteu ...gaega isseum nida.* ...명과 텐트...개가 있습니다.

Camping/backpacking equipment

(the diagram shows the numbered parts)

	can opener	*byeong ttagae*	병따개
	butane gas	*butan gaseu*	부탄 가스
	campfire	*kaempeu paieo/modakbul*	캠프파이어/모닥불
	hammer	*mangchi*	망치
	hammock	*geumul chimdae*	그물 침대
	bottle	*byeong*	병
	clothes pin	*ppallae jipge*	빨래집게
	clothes line	*ppallae jjul*	빨래 줄
	windbreak	*baram magi*	바람 막이
	camp bed	*yayeong chimdae*	야영 침대
	compass	*nachimban*	나침반
	corkscrew	*koreukeu magae ppobi*	코르크 마개 뽑이
	lighter	*raiteo/jeomhwagi*	라이터/점화기
	table	*takja*	탁자
	penknife	*jumeoni kal*	주머니칼
1	tool bag	*gonggu gabang*	공구 가방
2	gas cooker	*gaseu yori gigu*	가스 요리기구
3	groundsheet	*geura undeu shiteu*	그라운드시트
4	gas can	*gaseu yonggi*	가스 용기
5	folding chair	*jeobi uija*	접이 의자
6	insulated picnic box	*kuleo*	쿨러
7	airbed	*gonggi chimdae*	공기 침대
8	airbed pump	*gonggi chimae peulleogeu*	공기침대 플러그
9	mat	*kkalgae*	깔개
10	saucepan	*naembi/soseupaen*	냄비/소스팬
11	handle (pan)	*sonjabi naembi*	손잡이 냄비
12	backpack	*baenang*	배낭
13	rope	*ro peu*	로프
14	storm lantern	*jeondeung*	전등
15	tent	*tenteu/cheonmak*	텐트/천막
16	tent peg	*chunmak malttuk*	천막 말뚝
17	tent pole	*chunmak gidung*	천막 기둥
18	water bottle	*mulppyeong*	물병
19	flashlight	*son jeondeung*	손전등

Can we pick our own site?	*Uriga yayeong jireul jikjeop gollado doenayo?* 우리가 야영지를 직접 골라도 되나요?
Do you have a quiet spot for us?	*Jom joyonghan goseul channeun deyo?* 좀 조용한 곳을 찾는데요?
Do you have any other sites available?	*Dareun de e bin gosi innayo?* 다른 데에 빈 곳이 있나요?
It's too windy/sunny/shady here.	*Yeogin barami neomu bureoyo/haesbyeoti simhaeyo/geuneuri jyeoyo.* 여긴 바람이 너무 불어요/햇볕이심해요/그늘이 져요.
It's too crowded here.	*Yeogin neomu bokjap haeyo.* 여긴 너무 복잡해요.
The ground's too hard/uneven.	*Ttangi neomu dandan haeyo/ultung bultung haeyo.* 땅이 너무 단단해요/울퉁불퉁해요.
Do you have a level spot for the camper/trailer/folding trailer?	*Yayeong/idong jutaek/joripju taegeuro sayong halsu inneun pyeongpyeonghan gosi innayo?* 야영/이동주택/조립주택으로 사용할수 있는 평평한 곳이 있나요?
Could we have adjoining sites?	*Buteo inneun goseuro juseyo?* 붙어있는 곳으로 주세요?
How much is it per person/tent/car?	*Irindang/han tenteu dang/cha handae dang eolma ingayo?* 일인당/한 텐트 당/차 한대 당 얼마인가요?
Do you have chalets for hire?	*Imdae jungin byeoljjangi innayo?* 임대 중인 별장이 있나요?
Are there any...?	*...ga innayo?* ...가 있나요?
Are there any hot showers?	*Onsuga naoneun syawo siri innayo?* 온수가 나오는 샤워실이 있나요?
Are there any washing machines?	*Setak giga innayo?* 세탁기가 있나요?
Is there a...on the site?	*Yayeong ji e...ga innayo?* 야영지에...가 있나요?

Is there a children's play area on the site?	*Yayeong ji e nori teoga innayo?* 야영지에 놀이터가 있나요?
Are there covered cooking facilities on the site?	*Yayeong ji e yorisi seori innayo?* 야영지에 요리시설이 있나요?
Are we allowed to barbecue here?	*Babikyu reul haedo doenayo?* 바비큐를 해도 되나요?
Are there any power outlets?	*Jeonseon kkojeul dega isseoyo?* 전선 꽂을 데가 있어요?
Is there drinking water?	*Sigyong suga innayo?* 식용수가 있나요?
When's the garbage collected?	*Sseure gineun eonje chiwo ganayo?* 쓰레기는 언제 치워가나요?
Do you sell gas bottles (butane gas/ propane gas)?	*Gaseu tong (butan gaseu/peuropan gaseu) parayo?* 가스통(부탄 가스/프로판 가스) 팔아요?

8. Money matters

8.1 Banks
8.2 Settling the bill

8.1 Banks

Where can I find a bank around here?	*Eunhaengi i geuncheo eodi e isseoyo?* 은행이 이 근처 어디에 있어요?
Where can I find an ATM around here?	*Hyeongeum inchul giga i geuncheo eodi e isseoyo?* 현금인출기가 이 근처 어디에 있어요?
What are the charges for withdrawing money from this ATM?	*I hyeongeum inchul giro chulgeum hagineun biyongi eolma yeyo?* 이 현금인출기로 출금하기는 비용이 얼마예요?
Can I cash this...here?	*Yeogiseo i...bakkul su isseoyo?* 여기서 이...바꿀 수 있어요?
Can I withdraw money on my credit card here?	*Je sinyong kadeuro hyeongeum inchuri doenayo?* 제 신용 카드로 현금인출이 되나요?
What's the minimum/ maximum amount?	*Choeso/choedae hando aegi eolma yeyo?* 최소/최대 한도액이 얼마예요?
Can I get less/more than that?	*Geugeot boda jeokge inchuldo doenayo?* 그것보다 적게 인출도 되나요?
This is my bank account number.	*Ige je eunhaeng gyejwa beonho imnida.* 이게 제 은행 계좌 번호 입니다.
I'd like to change some money.	*Doneul jom bakkugo sipeun deyo.* 돈을 좀 바꾸고 싶은데요.
I'd like to change...Euros.	*Euroreul bakkugo sipeun deyo.* 유로를 바꾸고 싶은데요.
I'd like to change...dollars.	*Dalleoreul ...ro bakkugo sipeun deyo.* 달러를...로 바꾸고 싶은데요.

What's the exchange rate?	*Hwanyuri eotteotke doenayo?* 환율이 어떻게 되나요?
Could you give me some small bills/coins with it?	*Igeol jando neuro bakkwo juseyo?* 이걸 잔돈으로 좀 바꿔주세요?
This is not right.	*Ingeon matjiga anneun deyo.* 이건 맞지가 않는데요.

여기 서명해 주세요.	Sign here, please.
이거 작성해 주세요.	Fill this out, please
여권을 보여 주세요?	Could I see your passport, please?
신분증을 보여 주세요?	Could I see your identity card, please?
은행 카드를 보여 주세요?	Could I see your bank card, please?

8.2 Settling the bill

Could you put it on my bill?	*Je gyesan seo e poham sikyeo jusi gesseoyo?* 제 계산서에 포함시켜 주시겠어요?
Is the tip included?	*Tipdo poham doenayo?* 팁도 포함되나요?
Can I pay by…?	*…ro gyesan hago sipeun deyo?* …로 계산하고 싶은데요?
Can I pay by credit card?	*Sinyong kadeuro gyesan halkkeyo?* 신용카드로 계산할게요?
Can I pay with foreign currency?	*Oeguk hwaneuro gyesan haedo doenayo?* 외국환으로 계산해도 되나요?

You've given me too
  much/you haven't given
  me enough change.
	*Geoseureum doneul neomu mani
	jusyeo sseoyo/jandoneul deol
	jusyeon neyo.*
	거스름돈을 너무 많이 주셨어요/잔돈을
	덜 주셨네요.

Could you check this again, please?	*Igeo dasi chekeu hae ju sillaeyo?* 이거 다시 체크 해 주실래요?

Could I have a receipt, please?	*Yeongsujeung juseyo?*
	영수증 주세요?
I don't have enough money on me.	*Doni jom mojara neundeyo.*
	돈이 좀 모자라는데요.
This is for you.	*Yeogi isseum nida.*
	여기 있습니다.
Keep the change.	*Jandoneun geunyang gaji seyo.*
	잔돈은 그냥 가지세요.
Do you accept Mastercard/VISA/ American Express credit cards?	*Masteu kadeu/Bija/Ame rikan Ikseu peureseu shinyong kadeu reul badeu seyo?*
	매스터카드/비자/아메리칸 익스프레스 신용카드를 받으세요?

| 신용카드/외국 돈은 받지 않 습니다. | We don't accept credit cards/ foreign currency. |

9. Mail, Phone and Internet

9.1 Mail
9.2 Telephone
9.3 Internet

With the popularization of the Internet, a number of Internet cafes and so-called 'PC rooms' have appeared everywhere in Korea. There, people enjoy surfing on the sea of information or playing games with other netizens around the world, along with snacks and music.

Post offices in Korea have been diversifying their business areas. A variety of banking services are now available at more than 3,000 post offices across the nation. They also operate mail order services and issue some civil affairs documents.

Mailing services are divided mainly into two kinds: speed delivery and ordinary delivery. Speed delivery mail arrives within 1–2 days for about double the postal rates, while ordinary mail arrives within 2–4 days.

Mail

stamps	money orders	parcels	EMS
upyo	*upyeon hwan*	*sopo*	*gukje teuksong upyeon*
우표	우편환	소포	국제 특송 우편

Where is...?	*...eodi e isseoyo?*
	...어디에 있어요?
Where is the nearest post office?	*Gakka un uche gugi eodi e isseoyo?*
	가까운 우체국이 어디에 있어요?
Where is the main post office?	*Jungang uche gugi eodi e isseoyo?*
	중앙 우체국이 어디에 있어요?
Where is the nearest mail box?	*Gakka un uche tongi eodi e isseoyo?*
	가까운 우체통이 어디에 있어요?
Which counter should I go to?	*Eoneu changguro gamyeon doenayo?*
	어느 창구로 가면 되나요?

Which counter should I go to to send a fax?	*Pakseureul bonae ryeomyeon eoneu changguro gamyeon doenayo?* 팩스를 보내려면 어느 창구로 가면 되나요?
Which counter should I go to for general delivery?	*Ilban upyeon eun eoneu changguro gamyeon doenayo?* 일반 우편은 어느 창구로 가면 되나요?
Is there any mail for me?	*Jege on upyeon isseoyo?* 제게 온 우편있어요?
My name's...	*Je ireumeun...imnida* 제 이름은... 입니다

Stamps

What's the postage for ...to...?	*...eul...ro bonae neunde eolma deu reoyo?* ...을...로 보내는데 얼마 들어요?
Are there enough stamps on it?	*I upyoro chung bun haeyo?* 이 우표로 충분해요?
I'd like [value] [quantity] stamps.	*...jjari upyo...jang juseyo.* [Value] 짜리 우표 [quantity] 장 주세요.
I'd like to send this.	*Igeoseul bonae ryeogo haneun deyo.* 이것을 보내려고 하는데요.
I'd like to send this by express mail.	*Igeol ppa reun upyeo neuro bonae ryeogo haneun deyo.* 이걸 빠른우편으로 보내려고 하는데요.
I'd like to send this by air mail.	*Igeol hanggong upyeo neuro bonae ryeogo haneun deyo.* 이걸 항공우편으로 보내려고 하는데요.
I'd like to send this by registered mail.	*Igeol deung-giro bonae ryeogo haneun deyo.* 이걸 등기로 보내려고 하는데요.

EMS/fax

| I'd like to EMS. | *Gukje teuksong upyeo neul bonae ryeogo.*
국제 특송 우편을 보내려고 하는데요. |
| How much is it for...? | *...ro bonae neun de eolma yeyo?*
...로 보내는데 얼마예요? |

This is what I want to EMS.	*Igeoseul gukje teuksong upyeo neuro bonae ryeogo haeyo.* 이것을 국제 특송 우편으로 보내려고 해요.
Shall I fill out the form myself?	*Jega sseo neo eoya hanayo?* 제가 써 넣어야 하나요?
Can I make photocopies/ send a fax here?	*Yeogiseo boksa/paekseu halsu isseoyo?* 여기서 복사/팩스 할 수 있어요?
How much is it per page?	*Han pei jie eolma yeyo?* 한 페이지에 얼마예요?

Telephone

Direct international calls can easily be made from public telephones using a phone card available from newspaper stands or from vending machines next to the telephone booths. Phone cards have a value of 2,000 or 3,000 Won. Dial 001 or 002 to get out of Korea, then the relevant country code (USA 1), city code and number.

Is there a phone booth around here?	*Geuncheo-e gongjung jeonhwa isseoyo?* 근처에 공중 전화 있어요?
May I use your phone, please?	*Jeonhwa jom sseodo doel kkayo?* 전화 좀 써도 될까요?
Do you have a phone directory?	*Jeonhwa beonhobu gajigo gyeseyo?* 전화 번호부 가지고 계세요?
Where can I get a phone card?	*Jeonhwa kadeu reul eodiseo sanayo?* 전화카드를 어디서 사나요?
Could you give me...?	*...jom gareucheo juseyo?* ...좀 가르쳐 주세요?
Could you give me the number for international directory assistance?	*Gukje jeonhwa annae beonhoreul jom gareucheo juseyo?* 국제전화 안내번호를 좀 가르쳐 주세요?
Could you give me the number of room...?	*...sil jeonhwa beonhoreul jom gareucheo juseyo?* ...실 전화 번호를 좀 가르쳐 주세요?

Could you give me the international access code?	*Gukje jadong jeonhwa sik byeol beonho reul jom gareucheo juseyo?* 국제자동전화 식별번호를 좀 가르쳐 주세요?
Could you give me the country code?	*Gukka beonho reul jom gareucheo juseyo?* 국가 번호를 좀 가르쳐 주세요?
Could you give me the area code?	*Jiyeok beonho reul jom gareucheo juseyo?* 지역 번호를 좀 가르쳐 주세요?
Could you give me the number of [subscriber]…?	*…ui beonho reul jom gareucheo juseyo?* …의 번호를 좀 가르쳐 주세요?
Could you check if this number's correct?	*Beonhoga manneunji hwagin jom hae juseyo?* 번호가 맞는지 확인 좀 해 주세요?
Can I dial international direct?	*Gukje jiktong jeonhwa reul hal su innayo?* 국제 직통 전화를 할 수 있나요?
Do I have to go through the switchboard?	*Gyohwa neul bulleo ya doenayo?* 교환을 불러야 되나요?
Do I have to dial '0' first?	*Yeongbeoneul meonjeo nulleo ya hanayo?* 0 번을 먼저 눌러야 하나요?
Could you dial this number for me, please?	*I beonho ro jeonhwa jom hae jusil su isseoyo?* 이 번호로 전화 좀 해 주실 수 있어요?
Could you put me through to extension…, please?	*…beonuro yeongyeol hae juseyo?* …번으로 연결해 주세요?
I'd like to place a collect call to…	*…ege kollekt koreul haryeogo haeyo* …에게 콜렉트 콜을 하려고 해요
What's the charge per minute?	*Ilbune eolma yeyo?* 일 분에 얼마예요?
Have there been any calls for me?	*Jege jeonhwa on geo isseoyo?* 제게 전화 온 거 있어요?

The conversation

Hello, this is…	*Yeobo seyo, …imnida* 여보세요, …입니다
Who is this, please?	*Nugu seyo?* 누구세요?
Is this…?	*…iseyo?* …이세요?
I'm sorry, I've dialed the wrong number.	*Joesong hamnida, jal mot georeo sseoyo.* 죄송합니다, 잘 못 걸었어요.
I can't hear you.	*Jal an deulli neundeyo.* 잘 안 들리는 데요.
I'd like to speak to…	*…jom bakkwo juseyo* …좀 바꿔 주세요
Is there anybody who speaks English?	*Yeongeoreul hal jura neun buni gyeseyo?* 영어를 할 줄아는 분이 계세요?
Extension…, please.	*…beoneuro yeongyeol hae juseyo.* …번으로 연결해 주세요.
Could you ask him/her to call me back?	*…Ege jeonhwa hae dallago jeonhae juseyo?* [Person's name]…에게 전화해 달라고 전해주세요?
My name's…	*Je ireumeun … imnida* 제 이름은 … 입니다
My number's…	*Je jeonhwa beonho neun … imnida* 제 전화번호는…입니다
Could you tell him/her I called?	*Jega jeonhwa haetdago jeonhae juseyo?* 제가 전화했다고 전해주세요?
I'll call him/her back tomorrow.	*Naeil dasi jeonhwa halkeyo.* 내일 다시 전화할게요.

전화가 왔었습니다.	There's a phone call for you.
0 번을 먼저 누르세요.	You have to dial '0' first.

잠깐 기다리세요.	One moment, please.
응답이 없습니다.	There's no answer.
통화 중입니다.	The line's busy.
기다리시겠어요?	Do you want to hold?
연결 중입니다...	Connecting you...
잘 못 거셨습니다.	You've got a wrong number.
자리에 없습니다.	He's/she's not here right now.
잠시 후 돌아오실 겁니다.	He'll/she'll be back later.
...의 자동 응답기입니다	This is the answering machine of...

Mobile Phone

Please send me a
  text message.
Munja mesiji namgyeo juseyo.
문자 메시지 남겨 주세요.

I will send you a
  text message.
Munja mesiji namgil geyo.
문자 메시지 남길게요.

The (phone) connection
  is not good. It keeps
  being cut off.
*(Jeonhwa) yeonggyeol jal andwaeyo.
Jakku kkeuneo jyeoyo.*
(전화) 연결이 잘 안돼요. 자꾸 끊어져요.

I will send you the
  picture via WhatsApp/
  Line. What is your
  mobile number?
*Sajin eul Watcheuaep/Laineu robo
nael geyo. Haen deu pon beonho
neun mwo yeyo?*
사진을 왓츠앱/라인으로 보낼게요.
핸드폰 번호는 뭐예요?

Do you have this...app?
I ... aepeul innayo?
이 … 앱을 있나요?

beauty
byuti
뷰티

game
geim
게임

subway/train
jihacheol/kicha
지하철/기차

translation
beonyeok
번역

discounts/deals
halin
할인

fashion	*paesheon* 패션
Do you have…	*… innayo?* …있나요?
portable wifi router	*hyudaeyong wai pai rauteo* 휴대용 와이파이 라우터
portable charger	*hyudaeyong chung jeongi* 휴대용 충전기
Let's take a selfie!	*Selka reul haja!* 셀카를 하자!

9.3 Internet

I cannot get on the Internet.	*Internet yeongyeoli andwaeyo.* 인터넷 연결이 안돼요.
You can find it on Google.com.	*Google-ro chajeumyeon nawayo.* 구글로/찾으면 나와요.
Do you have a wireless connection here?	*Yeogi mu seon Internet dwaeyo?* 여기 무선 인터넷 돼요?
Do I need a password to connect to the Internet?	*Internet jeobsokha ryeomyeon amhoga piryo haeyo?* 인터넷 접속하려면 암호가 필요해요?
The Internet is very fast/slow.	*Internetsi aju ppallayo/neuryeoyo.* 인터넷이 아주 빨라요/느려요.

Social Media

Do you use Facebook/ Cyworld/Instagram?	*Peiseu bukeul/Ssai woldeureul/Inseu tageu raemeul sseoseyo?* 페이스북을/싸이월드를/인스타그램을 써세요?
What is your blog address?	*Blog jusoga eotteoke dwaeyo?* 블로그 주소가 어떻게 돼요?
I saved my photos in my computer.	*Sajineul compu tere jeojang haeseoyo.* 사진을 컴퓨터에 저장했어요.
I will email you these photos.	*Sajineul emailro bonae julgeyo.* 사진을 이메일로 보내 줄게요.

10. Shopping

10.1 Shopping conversations
10.2 Food
10.3 Clothing and shoes
10.4 Photographs and electronic goods
10.5 At the hairdresser

Major department stores are open from 10:30 a.m. until 8:00 p.m. including Sundays, but smaller shops are usually open until late evening every day. There are also 24-hour convenience stores available in major cities. You can converse in English in the shopping arcades of major hotels and certainly in Itaewon Market in Southern Seoul. Shops in Namdaemun Market and Dongdaemun Market in Seoul offer a variety of goods at bargain prices. There are 24-hour shops in Seoul, especially in the main shopping belts.

barber *ibalgwan* 이발관	watches and clocks *sigyejeom* 시계점	market *sijang* 시장
coin-operated laundry *ppallaebang* 빨래방	furniture shop *gagujeom* 가구점	florist *kkotjip* 꽃집
confectioners/ cake shop *satang/keikeu jeonmunjeom* 사탕/케이크 전문점	fruit and vegetable shop *cheong gwamulsang* 청과물상	household appliances *gajeon jepum* 가전제품
grocery shop *sigpumjeom* 식품점	second-hand shop *jung gosang* 중고상	fishmonger *saengseon gage* 생선가게
book shop *seojeom* 서점	optician *angyeongjeom* 안경점	beauty salon/ hairdresser *miyongsil* 미용실
toy shop *jangnangam gage* 장난감가게	costume jewelry *injo boseog* 인조 보석	pharmacy *yaggug* 약국

baker's shop, bakery
ppangjib
빵집

musical instrument
 shop
aggijeom
악기점

footwear/shoe shop
sinbal gage
신발가게

hardware shop
cheolmuljeom
철물점

shoe repair
gudu suseon
구두수선

stationery shop
mungujeom
문구점

fabric shop
pomog jeom
포목점

motorbike/bicycle
 repairs
*otoboai/jajeongeo suli
 jeom*
오토바이/자전거
 수리점

dry cleaners
hwawon
화원

butcher
jeong yukjeom
정육점

newsstand
sinmun gapandae
신문 가판대

ice cream shop
aiseu keulim gage
아이스크림가게

department store
baeghwa jeom
백화점

camera shop
kamela jeom
카메라점

sporting goods
undong gujeom
운동구점

leather goods
gajug jeonmun jeom
가죽전문점

greengrocer
cheong gwamulsang
청과물상

goldsmith
geumsegong
금세공

perfumery
*hwangsujeon
 munjeom*
향수전문점

delicatessen
delli gage
델리가게

laundry
setagso
세탁소

jeweler
boseogsang
보석상

supermarket
syupeo maket
슈퍼마켓

nursery (plants)
hwawon
화원

hardware store
cheolmul jeom
철물점

10.1 Shopping conversations

Where can I get...?	*...eodi e isseoyo?* ...어디에 있어요?
When is this shop open?	*I gage myeot sikkaji yeo reoyo?* 이 가게 몇 시까지 열어요?
Could you tell me where the ... department is?	*...maejang eodi e isseoyo?* ...매장 어디에 있어요?

Could you help me, please?	*Yeogi jom bwa jusi gesseoyo?* 여기 좀 봐 주시겠어요?
I'm looking for …	*...chatgo inneun deyo* ...찾고 있는데요
Do you sell English/ American newspapers?	*Yeongja sinmun isseoyo?* 영자 신문 있어요?

도와 드릴까요?	Are you being served?
또 필요하신 거 없으세요?	Anything else?

No, I'd like…	*Anyo, ...eul/reul juseyo.* 아뇨, ...을/를 주세요.
I'm just looking, if that's all right.	*Geunyang gugyeong haneun jung ieyo.* 그냥 구경하는 중이에요.
Yes, I'd also like …	*Ne, ...do juseyo* 네, ...도 주세요
No, thank you. That's all.	*Anyo, gwaencha nayo. Geuge jeonbu yeoyo.* 아뇨, 괜찮아요. 그게 전부예요.
Could you show me …?	*...jom boyeo jusi gesseoyo?* ...좀 보여 주시겠어요?
I'd prefer …	*...ga deo joayo* ...가 더 좋아요
This is not what I'm looking for.	*Igeo jega channeun geo ani yeoyo.* 이거 제가 찾는 거 아니예요.
It's too expensive.	*Neomu bissayo.* 너무 비싸요.
Thank you, I'll keep looking.	*Gamsa hamnida, jom deo gugyeong hage sseoyo.* 감사합니다, 좀 더 구경하겠어요.
Do you have something …?	*...geo isseoyo?* ...거 있어요?
less expensive	*deol bissan* 덜 비싼

smaller	*deo jageun* 더 작은
larger	*deo keun* 더 큰
I'll take this one.	*Igeo sage sseoyo.* 이거 사겠어요.
Does it come with instructions?	*Seolmyeong seodo gachi innayo?* 설명서도 같이 있나요?
I'll give you …	*…deuri gesseoyo* …드리겠어요
Could you keep this for me?	*Igeo jom bogwanhae jusi gesseoyo?* 이거 좀 보관해 주시겠어요?
I'll come back for it later.	*Najunge gajireo o gesseoyo.* 나중에 가지러 오겠어요.
Do you have a bag for me, please?	*Syoping baek hana jusi gesseoyo?* 쇼핑백 하나 주시겠어요?
Could you gift wrap it, please?	*Igeo seonmul pojang jom hae jusi gesseoyo?* 이거 선물포장 좀 해 주시겠어요?

죄송합니다, 없습니다.	I'm sorry, we don't have that.
죄송합니다, 매진입니다.	I'm sorry, we're sold out.
죄송합니다, … 까지는 안 들어옵니다	I'm sorry, it won't come back in until…
계산대에서 지불하세요.	Please pay at the cash register.
신용카드 안 받습니다.	We don't accept credit cards.
외국돈 안 받습니다.	We don't accept foreign currency.

10.2 Food

I'd like a hundred grams of …, please	*…baek geuram juseyo* … 백그람 주세요
I'd like half a kilo/five hundred grams of …	*…ban kiro/…o baek geuram juseyo* … 반 키로/…오백그람 주세요

I'd like a kilo of...	*...il kiro juseyo*
	...일키로 주세요
Could you ... it for me, please?	*...jom jusi gesseoyo?*
	...좀 주시겠어요?
slice it/cut it up for me, please?	*sseoreo/jalla jusi gesseoyo?*
	썰어/잘라 주시겠어요?
grate it for me, please?	*gara jusi gesseoyo?*
	갈아 주시겠어요?
Can I order it?	*Jumun hal su isseoyo?*
	주문할 수 있어요?
I'll pick it up tomorrow/ at ...	*Naeil/... si e gajireo o gesseoyo*
	내일/... 시에 가지러 오겠어요
Can you eat/drink this?	*Igeo meogeul su/masil su isseoyo?*
	이거 먹을 수/마실 수 있어요?
What's in it?	*Geu ane mwoga deureo sseoyo?*
	그 안에 뭐가 들었어요?

10.3 Clothing and shoes

I saw something in the window.	*Syo windou eseo mwol jom bwasseoyo.*
	쇼 윈도우에서 뭘 좀 봤어요.
Shall I point it out?	*Garikye deuril kkayo?*
	가리켜 드릴까요?
I'd like something to go with this.	*Igeo hago eoul lineun geol sago sipeoyo.*
	이거하고 어울리는 걸 사고 싶어요.
Do you have shoes to match this?	*Igeo hago eoul lineun sinbal isseoyo?*
	이거하고 어울리는 신발 있어요?
I'm a size ... in the US.	*Miguk sigeuro saijeu... ieyo.*
	미국식으로 사이즈... 이에요.
Can I try this on?	*Igeo ibeo (clothing) /sineo (shoes) bwado dwaeyo?*
	이거 입어(clothing)/신어(shoes)봐도 돼요?
Where's the fitting room?	*Tari sili eodi e isseoyo?*
	탈의실이 어디에 있어요?

It doesn't suit me.	*Jeoege an majayo.* 저에게 안 맞아요.
This is the right size.	*Ige manneun saijeu yeyo.* 이게 맞는 사이즈예요.
It doesn't look good on me.	*Jeoege an eoul lyeoyo.* 저에게 안 어울려요.
Do you have this/these in …(size, color)?	*Igeo… ro isseoyo?* 이거…로 있어요?
The heels are too high/low.	*Gubi neomu nopayo/najayo.* 굽이 너무 높아요/낮아요.
Is this real leather?	*Igeo jinjja gajugi eyo?* 이거 진짜 가죽이에요?
I'm looking for a … for a …-year-old child.	*(Age)… saljjari eori niyong (item)… eul/reul chatgo isseoyo.* (Age)… 살짜리 어린이용 (item)…을/를 찾고 있어요.
I'd like a …	*…eul/reul sago sipeoyo* …을/를 사고 싶어요
silk	*silkeu* 실크
cotton	*myeon* 면
woolen	*ul* 울
linen	*rinnen* 린넨
At what temperature should I wash it?	*Myeot do e setak aeya haeyo?* 몇 도에 세탁해야 해요?
Will it shrink in the wash?	*Setak hu e jureodeu reoyo?* 세탁 후에 줄어들어요?

| Hand wash
Son setag
손세탁 | Do not iron.
Dariji maseyo.
다리지 마세요. | Do not spin dry.
Talsugiro jjaji maseyo.
탈수기로 짜지 마세요. |
| Dry clean
Deulai keullining
드라이 클리닝 | Machine washable
Gigye setag ganeung
기계세탁 가능 | Lay flat
Nwieoseo malli seyo
뉘어서 말리세요 |

At the cobbler

Could you mend these shoes?	*I gudu jom gochyeo jusi gesseoyo?* 이 구두 좀 고쳐 주시겠어요?
Could you resole/reheel these shoes?	*I gudu mitchang/gup jom gara jusi gesseoyo?* 이 구두 밑창/굽 좀 갈아 주시겠어요?
When will they be ready?	*Eonje doel kkayo?* 언제 될까요?
I'd like…, please	*… jom juseyo* …좀 주세요
a can of shoe polish	*gudu yak han tong* 구두약 한 통
a pair of shoelaces	*gudu kkeun han beol* 구두끈 한 벌

10.4 Photographs and electronic goods

I'd like batteries for this (digital) camera.	*I kame rae deureo ganeun baeteo rireul juseyo.* 이 카메라에 들어가는 배터리를 주세요.
I'd like a 64gb memory card, please.	*Kateu ritji hana juseyo.* 카트릿지 하나 주세요.
Two AA batteries, please.	*AA baeteori du gae juseyo.* AA 배터리 두 개 주세요.
May I have a USB flash drive?	*USB memori kadeu juseyo?* USB 메모리 카드 주세요?
Please scan the document and email it to me.	*Geu munseo reul scan haeseo bonae juseyo.* 그 문서를 스캔해서 보내 주세요.

Problems

Because the size of the photo is too big, I will have to compress it.	*Sajinui yongnyangi neomu keoseo keugi reul jureoya haeyo.* 사진의 용량이 너무 커서 크기를 줄여야 해요.

Please delete/copy the photo.	*Sajineul sakje/boksa haseyo.* 사진을 삭제/복사 하세요.
Can you put in the batteries for me, please?	*Baeteori jom neoeo jusi gesseoyo?* 배터리 좀 넣어 주시겠어요?
Should I replace the batteries?	*Batderi reul garaya hamnikka?* 밧데리를 갈아야 합니까?
Could you have a look at my camera, please?	*Je kamera jom bwa jusi gesseoyo?* 제 카메라 좀 봐 주시겠어요?
It's not working.	*Jadongi an dwaeyo.* 작동이 안 돼요.
The ... is broken	*...i/ga gojang nasseoyo* ...이/가 고장났어요
The camera memory is full.	*Memori ga da dwaeseoyo.* 메모리가 다 됐어요.
I need to change the memory card.	*Memori kadeu reul garaya dwaeyo.* 메모리 카드를 갈아야 돼요.
The flash isn't working.	*Peullae swiga andwaeyo.* 플래쉬가 안돼요.
My computer ran out of battery.	*Je computer bateori ga da dwaeseoyo.* 제 컴퓨터 배터리가 다 됐어요.
There is a hardware/software problem with the computer.	*Computer hadeu we eoe/sopeuteu we eoe munjega isseoyo.* 컴퓨터 하드웨어에/소프트웨어에 문제가 있어요.

Processing and prints

I'd like to have these pictures printed, please.	*I pilleum hyeonsang/inhwa jom hae juseyo.* 이 필름 현상/인화 좀 해 주세요.
I'd like ... prints from each of these pictures.	*Jeonbu... jangssik ppoba juseyo.* 전부 ... 장씩 뽑아주세요.
glossy/matte	*gwangtaek ji/maeteu ji* 광택지/매트지
6 x 9	*yuk gu inchi saijeu* 육 구 인치 사이즈

I'd like to order reprints of these photos.	*I sajin jom deo ppoba juseyo.* 이 사진 좀 더 뽑아 주세요.
I'd like to have this photo enlarged.	*I sajin jom hwakdae hae juseyo.* 이 사진 좀 확대 해 주세요.
How much is processing/printing?	*Sajin cheori neun/inhwaha neun de eolma yeyo?* 사진 처리는/인화하는 데 얼마예요?
How much are the reprints?	*Deo ppom neun de eolma yeyo?* 더 뽑는 데 얼마예요?
How much is it for enlargement?	*Hwakdaeha neun de eolma yeyo?* 확대하는 데 얼마예요?
When will they be ready?	*Eonje doel kkayo?* 언제 될까요?

10.5 At the hairdresser

Do I have to make an appointment?	*Yeyak haeya dwaeyo?* 예약해야 돼요?
Can I come in right now?	*Jigeum dangjang gado dwaeyo?* 지금 당장 가도 돼요?
How long will I have to wait?	*Eolma dongan gida ryeoya doel kkayo?* 얼마동안 기다려야 될까요?
I'd like a shampoo/haircut.	*Syampu/keoteu jom hae juseyo.* 샴푸/컷트 좀 해 주세요.
I'd like a shampoo for oily/dry hair, please.	*Jiseong/geonseong meo ri yong syampu jom hae juseyo.* 지성/건성 머리용 샴푸 좀 해 주세요.
I'd like an anti-dandruff shampoo.	*Bideum syampu jom hae juseyo.* 비듬 샴푸 좀 해 주세요.
I'd like a color-rinse shampoo, please.	*Yeomsaek jeonyong syampu jom hae juseyo.* 염색전용 샴푸 좀 해 주세요.
I'd like a shampoo with conditioner, please.	*Rinseu gyeomyong syampu jom hae juseyo.* 린스겸용 샴푸 좀 해 주세요.
I'd like highlights, please.	*Beullichi jom neoeo juseyo.* 블리치 좀 넣어주세요.

Do you have a color chart, please?	*Kalla gyeonbon isseoyo?* 칼라 견본 있어요?
I'd like to keep the same color.	*Jigeum hago gateun saegeuro jom hae juseyo.* 지금하고 같은 색으로 좀 해 주세요.
I'd like it darker/lighter.	*Deo eodeupge/balkke jom hae juseyo.* 더 어둡게/밝게 좀 해 주세요.
I'd like/I don't want hairspray.	*He eo seupeurei hae juseyo/haji maseyo.* 헤어 스프레이 해 주세요/하지 마세요.
gel/lotion	*jel/rosyeon* 젤/로션
I'd like short bangs.	*Ammeori jjalkke jom hae juseyo.* 앞머리 짧게 좀 해 주세요.
Not too short at the back.	*Dwineun neomu jjaljji anke hae juseyo.* 뒤는 너무 짧지 않게 해 주세요.
Not too long.	*Neomu gil ji anke hae juseyo.* 너무 길지 않게 해 주세요.
I'd like it curly/not too curly.	*Gopseul gopseul hage/neomu gopseul gopseul haji anke jom hae juseyo.* 곱슬곱슬하게/너무 곱슬곱슬하지 않게 좀 해 주세요.
It needs a little/a lot taken off.	*Yak gan/mani jom chyeo juseyo.* 약간/많이 좀 쳐 주세요.
I'd like a completely different style/cut.	*Wanjeonhi dareun seuta illo/keoteuro jom hae juseyo.* 완전히 다른 스타일로/컷트로 좀 해 주세요.
I'd like it the same as in this photo.	*I sajin cheoreom jom hae juseyo.* 이 사진처럼 좀 해 주세요.
as that woman's	*jeo yeoja cheoreom* 저 여자처럼
Could you turn the drier up/down a bit?	*Deurai eo jom ollyeo/naeryeo jusi gesseoyo?* 드라이어 좀 올려/내려 주시겠어요?
I'd like a facial.	*Eolgul sonjil jom hae juseyo.* 얼굴 손질 좀 해 주세요.

a manicure	*sontop sonjil* 손톱 손질
a massage	*masaji* 마사지
Could you trim my…, please?	*Je… jom dadeumeo jusi gesseoyo?* 제 … 좀 다듬어 주시겠어요?
bangs	*ammeori* 앞머리
beard	*teok suyeom* 턱수염
moustache	*kot suyeom* 콧수염
I'd like a shave, please.	*Myeondo jom hae juseyo.* 면도 좀 해주세요.

어떻게 잘라 드릴까요?	How do you want it cut?
무슨 스타일을 원하세요?	What style did you have in mind?
무슨 칼라를 원하세요?	What color did you want it?
온도가 괜찮으세요?	Is the temperature all right for you?
읽을 거 드릴까요?	Would you like something to read?
마실 거 드릴까요?	Would you like a drink?
이게 원하시던 거예요?	Is this what you had in mind?

Excuse me, where is the Tourist Information Center?
Sillye hamnida. Gwangwang annae soga eodi e isseoyo?

Thank you for your help.
Dang sinui doumeui jusyeoseo gamsa hamnida.

It's over there, straight ahead and then turn right.
Jeojjoge, ddok baro, wheejeon geuligo.

Hi, how can I help you?
Annyeong haseyo. Eotteoke dowa deuli kkayo?

Hello. Do you have a city map? What are the main places of interest here?
Annyeong haseyo. Sinae jido isseoyo? Gwangwang myeong soga eodi yeyo?

11. Tourist Activities

11.1 Places of interest
11.2 Going out
11.3 Booking tickets

Tourist information and assistance can easily be obtained from the Tourist Information Center (TIC) of the Korea National Tourism Organization (KNTO)—open every day from 9 a.m. to 8.pm. (82-2-7299-497-499)—in Seoul. These are also available from the Seoul City Tourist Information Centers at major tourist attractions in Seoul, or from the information counters at the three international airports (Incheon, Gimhae, and Jeju), or from major transportation terminals such as railway stations, ferry or bus terminals in major cities. There is also the Korea Travel Phone service (call 1330) offering tourist information and assistance in English.

11.1 Places of interest

War Memorial of Korea
Jeongjaeng Gimyeomgwan
전쟁기념관

N Seoul Tower
Nseoul Tawo
N 서울타워

Seoraksan National Park
Seolagsan Gungnip Gongwon
설악산 국립 공원

Korean Folk Village
Hangug Minsog Maeul
한국 민속 마을

Demilitarized Zone
Bimujang Jidae
비무장 지대

Jamsil Baseball Stadium
Jamsil Yagu Gyeonggijang
잠실 야구 경기장

National Museum of Korea
Gungnipjung Angbag Mulgwan
국립중앙박물관

Where's the Tourist Information Center?
Gwangwang annae soga eodi e isseoyo?
관광 안내소가 어디에 있어요?

Do you have a city map?	*Sinae jido isseoyo?* 시내 지도 있어요?
Where is the museum?	*Bangmul gwani eodi e isseoyo?* 박물관이 어디에 있어요?
Where can I find a church?	*Gyohoega eodi e isseoyo?* 교회가 어디에 있어요?
Could you give me some information about …?	*…e daehae seo annae jom hae jusi gesseoyo?* …에 대해서 안내 좀 해 주시겠어요?
How much is this?	*Igeo eolma yeyo?* 이거 얼마예요?
What are the main places of interest?	*Gwangwang myeong soga eodi yeyo?* 관광명소가 어디예요?
What do you recommend?	*Eodi reul chucheon hasi gesseoyo?* 어디를 추천하시겠어요?
We'll be here for a few hours.	*Yeogi du se sigan isseul geo yeyo.* 여기 두 세 시간 있을 거예요.
We'll be here for a day.	*Yeogi haru isseul geo yeyo.* 여기 하루 있을 거예요.
We'll be here for a week.	*Yeogi il juil isseul geo yeyo.* 여기 일주일 있을 거예요.
We're interested in…	*…e gwansimi isseoyo* …에 관심이 있어요
Is there a scenic walk around the city?	*Sinae geuncheo e jeon mangi joeun sanchaeng no isseoyo?* 시내 근처에 전망이 좋은 산책로 있어요?
How long does it take?	*Eolmana geollyeoyo?* 얼마나 걸려요?
Where does it start/end?	*Eodi eseo sijak dwaeyo/kkeun nayo?* 어디에서 시작돼요/끝나요?
Are there any boat trips?	*Yuramseon tueo isseoyo?* 유람선 투어 있어요?
Where can we board?/ get on?	*Eodi eseo tayo?* 어디에서 타요?
Are there any bus tours?	*Gwangwang beoseu tueoga isseoyo?* 관광버스 투어가 있어요?

Is there a guide who speaks English?	*Yeongeohal jul aneun gaideu isseoyo?* 영어 할 줄 아는 가이드 있어요?
What trips can we take around the area?	*Geu jiyeoge eotteon tueoga isseoyo?* 그 지역에 어떤 투어가 있어요?
Are there any excursions?	*Ya oe tueoga isseoyo?* 야외 투어가 있어요?
Where do they go to?	*Eodi ro gayo?* 어디로 가요?
We'd like to go to …	*…e gago sipeoyo* …에 가고 싶어요
How long is the excursion?	*Geu tueo neun eolmana geolyeoyo?* 그 투어는 얼마나 걸려요?
How long do we stay in…?	*…e eolmana o rae isseoyo?* …에 얼마나 오래 있어요?
Are there any guided tours?	*Gaideu tueoga isseoyo?* 가이드 투어가 있어요?
How much free time will we have there?	*Geogi eso jayu sigani eolmana isseoyo?* 거기에서 자유시간이 얼마나 있어요?
We want to have a walk around/to go on foot.	*Georeoso danigo sipeoyo.* 걸어서 다니고 싶어요.
Can we hire a guide?	*Gaideu reul goyonghal su isseoyo?* 가이드를 고용할 수 있어요?
What time does … open/close?	*Myeot si e …yeo reoyo/dadayo?* 몇 시에 …열어요/닫아요?
What days is … open/closed?	*Museun yoire …yeo reoyo/dadayo?* 무슨 요일에 …열어요/닫아요?
What's the admission price?	*Ipjang nyoga eolma yeyo?* 입장료가 얼마예요?
Is there a group discount?	*Danche harin dwaeyo?* 단체 할인 돼요?
Is there a child discount?	*Eorini harin dwaeyo?* 어린이 할인 돼요?
Is there a discount for senior citizens?	*Gyeongno harin dwaeyo?* 경로 할인 돼요?
Can I take (flash) photos here?	*(Peullaeswi) sajin jjigeodo dwaeyo?* (플래쉬) 사진 찍어도 돼요?

Do you have any postcards of …?	*…yeopseo isseoyo?* …엽서 있어요?
Do you have an English …?	*Yeongeo …isseoyo?* 영어 …있어요?
catalog	*kata rogeu* 카타로그
program	*peuro geuraem* 프로그램
brochure	*beuro syueo* 브로슈어

11.2 Going out

Do you have this week's/month's entertainment guide?	*Ibeon ju/dal gongyeon annaeseo isseoyo?* 이번 주/달 공연 안내서 있어요?
What's on tonight?	*Oneul jeonyeoge mwo haeyo?* 오늘 저녁에 뭐 해요?
We want to go to...	*…e gago sipeoyo* …에 가고 싶어요
What's on at the cinema?	*Geukjang eseo mwo haeyo?* 극장에서 뭐 해요?
What sort of film is that?	*Eotteon yeong hwa yeyo?* 어떤 영화예요?
suitable for everyone	*nuguna bol su inneun* 누구나 볼 수 있는
not suitable for people under 18	*yeolyeo deop sal ihaneun bol su eopneun* 열여덟 살 이하는 볼 수 없는
original version	*ori jinal pan* 오리지날 판
subtitled	*jamagi naoneun* 자막이 나오는
dubbed	*deobingi doen* 더빙이 된

Is it a continuous showing?	*Yeonsok sangyeong ieyo?* 연속상영이에요?
What's on at…?	*...eseo neun mwo haeyo?* …에서는 뭐 해요?
the theater	*geukjang* 극장
the opera	*opera geukjang* 오페라 극장
Where can I find a good nightclub around here?	*i geuncheo eseo joeun naiteu keulleobi eodi e isseoyo?* 이 근처에서 좋은 나이트 클럽이 어디에 있어요?
What's happening in the concert hall?	*Konseoteu hore seoneun mwo haeyo?* 콘서트 홀에서는 뭐 해요?
Is it members only?	*Hoewon jeonyong ieyo?* 회원 전용이에요?
Is it evening wear only?	*Yaho e bogeul kkok ibeo ya dwaeyo?* 야회복을 꼭 입어야 돼요?
Should I/we dress up?	*Jeong jang eul ibeo ya dwaeyo?* 정장을 입어야 돼요?
What time does the show start?	*Myeot si e gong yeoni sijak dwaeyo?* 몇 시에 공연이 시작돼요?
When's the next soccer match?	*Daeum chugu gyeongga eonje isseoyo?* 다음 축구경기가 언제 있어요?
I'd like an escort for tonight.	*Oneul jeonyeoge pateu neoga piryo haeyo.* 오늘 저녁에 파트너가 필요해요.
Is there a cover charge for entry into this bar?	*I baro ga neunde bongsa ryoga innayo?* 이 바로 가는데 봉사료가 있나요?
Is it Ladies' Night?	*Leidi jeu naiteu ingayo?* 레이디즈 나이트인가요?
What is your recommended/ signature drink?	*Chucheonhal manhan eumnyoga mwo yeyo?* 추천할 만한 음료가 뭐예요?
Can I try this *soju/maekgolli*?	*I soju/makgeolli reul masyeo bwado dwaeyo?* 이 소주/막걸리를 마셔 봐도 돼요?

When is the next baseball game?	*Daeum yagu geimeul eonje yeyo?* 다음 야구게임을 언제예요?
Who is playing?	*Museun timi gyeong gireul haeyo?* 무슨 팀이 경기를 해요?
"Korea!"	*Daehan minguk!* 대한민국!
Do you have any drinks with tequila/rum/vodka?	*Tekilla/reomju/bodeuka gadeuleo ganeun eumnyoga innayo?* 테킬라/럼주/보드카가 들어가는 음료가 있나요?
I can't drink alcohol. I'll have a Coke.	*Suleul anmeo geoyo. Kokeu reul halgeyo.* 술을 안 먹어요. 코크로 할게요.
What cocktail would you recommend? I like…	*Museun kakte ileul chucheon haseyo? Jega ...reul/eul joa haeyo* 무슨 칵테일을 추천하세요? 제가 ...를/을 좋아해요
sweet drinks	*daneumnyo* 단 음료
champagne	*syampein* 샴페인
What musical/opera/theatre show would you recommend?	*Museun myuji keoleul/opera reul/ yeongeukeul chucheon haseyo?* 무슨 뮤지컬을/오페라를/연극을 추천하세요?
Are the songs sung in Korean/English?	*Norae reul hanguk eoro/yeongeoro haeyo?* 노래를 한국어로/영어로 해요?
Are there any special exhibitions in the museums now?	*Jigeum bakmul gwane museun teukbyeol jeonshi hoega innayo?* 지금 박물관에 무슨 특별 전시회가 있나요?

11.3 Booking tickets

| Could you reserve some tickets for us? | *Tike teul myeot jang yeyakhae jusi gesseoyo?* 티켓을 몇 장 예약해 주시겠어요? |

We'd like to book… seats/a table for…	*Jwaseok …gae/…inyong teibeul* *hana reul yeyak hago sipeoyo* 좌석 …개/…인용 테이블 하나를 예약하고 싶어요
…seats in the orchestra in the main section	*okeseu teura …jang* 오케스트라석 …장
a box for…	*…inyong bakseu seok hana* …인용 박스석 하나
…seats in the middle/a table in the middle	*jung gan jwaseok …jang/jung gan* *teibeul hana* 중간 좌석 …장/중간 테이블 하나
…back row seats/a table at the back	*dwitjul jwaseok …jang/dwijjok* *teibeul hana* 뒷줄 좌석 …장/뒤쪽 테이블 하나
…front row seats/a table for…at the front	*apjul jwaseok …jang/…inyong apjjok* *teibeul hana* 앞줄 좌석 …장/…인용 앞쪽 테이블 하나
Could I reserve…seats for the…o'clock performance?	*…si gongyeon jwaseok …jang yeyakhae* *jusi gesseoyo?* …시 공연 좌석 …장 예약해 주시겠어요?
Are there any seats left for tonight?	*Oneul jeonyeok jwaseok nameun* *geo isseoyo?* 오늘 저녁 좌석 남은 거 있어요?
How much is a ticket?	*Tiket han jange eolma yeyo?* 티켓 한 장에 얼마예요?
When can I pick up the tickets?	*Eonje tiket chajeureo galkkayo?* 언제 티켓 찾으러 갈까요?
I've got a reservation.	*Yeyakhae sseoyo.* 예약했어요.

12. Sports Activities

12.1 Sporting questions
12.2 By the waterfront
12.3 In the snow

Many beaches, lakes and rivers like the Han River in Seoul offer a wide range of summer sports such as water skiing and canoeing. Scuba diving is popular on Jeju Island. Most travel agencies will operate bus trips between Seoul and several world-class ski resorts from mid December until early March. The most popular spectator sports are baseball and soccer.

12.1 Sporting questions

mountain climbing *deungsan* 등산	skiing *seuki tagi* 스키 타기	baseball *yagu* 야구
soccer *chugu* 축구	golf *golpeu* 골프	water skiing *susang seuki* 수상 스키

Where can we … around here?	*I geuncheo eodi eseo (eu)l su isseoyo?* 이 근처 어디에서 …(으)ㄹ 수 있어요?
Can we hire a …?	*…billil su isseoyo?* …빌릴 수 있어요?
Can we take … lessons?	*…gangseup badeul su isseoyo?* …강습 받을 수 있어요?
How much is that per hour/per day?	*Sigane/haru e eolma yeyo?* 시간에/하루에 얼마예요?
How much is each one?	*Gak gak eolma yeyo?* 각 각 얼마예요?
Do you need a permit for that?	*Heoga reul badaya dwaeyo?* 허가를 받아야 돼요?
Where can I get the permit?	*Eodi eseo heoga reul badeul su isseoyo?* 어디에서 허가를 받을 수 있어요?

12.2 By the waterfront

Is it far (to walk) to the sea?	*Bada kkaji (geot gi e) meo reoyo?* 바다까지 (걷기에) 멀어요?
Is there a…around here?	*I geuncheo e …isseoyo?* 이 근처에 …있어요?
a swimming pool	*suyeong jang* 수영장
a sandy beach	*morae sajang* 모래 사장
mooring place	*seonchak jang* 선착장
Are there any sunken rocks here?	*Yeogi amchoga isseoyo?* 여기 암초가 있어요?
When is high/low tide?	*Sseol muri/mil muri eonje yeyo?* 썰물이/밀물이 언제예요?
What's the water temperature?	*Suonneun eotteoke dwaeyo?* 수온은 어떻게 돼요?
Is it (very) deep here?	*Yeogi (aju) gipeoyo?* 여기 (아주) 깊어요?
Is it safe (for children) to swim here?	*Yeogi (eorin iga) suyeong hagiga anjeon haeyo?* 여기 (어린이가) 수영하기가 안전해요?
Are there any currents?	*Mulsari ganghan gosi isseoyo?* 물살이 강한 곳이 있어요?
Are there any rapids/ waterfalls along this river?	*I gange geum nyuga/pokpoga isseoyo?* 이 강에 급류가/폭포가 있어요?
What does that flag/ buoy mean?	*Jeo gitbari/bupyoga museun tteusi eyo?* 저 깃발이/부표가 무슨 뜻이에요?
Is there a lifeguard on duty?	*Inmyeong gujo woni isseoyo?* 인명 구조원이 있어요?
Are dogs allowed here?	*Yeogi gaereul derigo wado dwaeyo?* 여기 개를 데리고 와도 돼요?
Is camping on the beach allowed?	*Badat gaeseo kaemping haedo dwaeyo?* 바닷가에서 캠핑해도 돼요?

Fishing waters *Nakksiteo* 낚시터	No surfing *Seoping geumji* 서핑금지	No swimming *Suyeong geumji* 수영금지
Permits only *Myeonheo soji jajae hanham* 면허소지자자에 한함	Danger *Wiheom* 위험	No fishing *Nakksi geumji* 낚시금지

12.3 In the snow

Can I take ski lessons here?	*Yegi eseo seuki gangseup badeul su isseoyo?* 여기에서 스키강습 받을 수 있어요?
for beginners/ intermediate/advanced	*chogeup/junggeup/gogeup* 초급/중급/고급
How large are the groups?	*Bani eolmana keoyo?* 반이 얼마나 커요?
What languages are the classes in?	*Gangseu beseo eotteon eoneoreul sseoyo?* 강습에서 어떤 언어를 써요?
I'd like a lift pass, please.	*Ripeuteu paeseu hana juseyo.* 리프트 패스 하나 주세요.
Where are the beginner's slopes?	*Chogeup koseu neun eodi e isseoyo?* 초급 코스는 어디에 있어요?
Are there any cross-country ski runs around here?	*Keuroseu kanchyuri koseuga isseoyo?* 크로스 칸츄리 코스가 있어요?
Have the cross-country runs been marked?	*Keuroseu kanchyuri koseu e pyosiga isseoyo?* 크로스 칸츄리 코스에 표시가 있어요?
Are the ... open?	*...yeoreoss seoyo?* ...열었어요?
the ski lifts/chair lifts	*seuki ripeuteu/ripeuteu* 스키 리프트/리프트
the runs / cross country runs	*koseu/keuroseu kanchyuri koseu* 코스/크로스 칸츄리 코스

13. Health Matters

13.1 Calling a doctor
13.2 What's wrong?
13.3 The consultation
13.4 Medications and prescriptions
13.5 At the dentist

You can see any specialist or doctor without a GP's referral. Most doctors in hospitals in Korea speak some basic English. However, if you are in Seoul, it is recommended that you see the doctors in the International Clinics of general hospitals such as the Severance Hospital, Asan Medical Centre, or Samsung Medical Centre. You can buy medication for common illnesses over the counter at pharmacists without a doctor's prescription.

13.1 Calling a doctor

Could you call a doctor quickly, please?	*Uisa jom ppalli bulleo jusi gesseoyo?* 의사 좀 빨리 불러 주시겠어요?
When is the doctor in?	*Jillyo sigani eotteoke dwaeyo?* 진료시간이 어떻게 돼요?
When can the doctor come?	*Eonje uisaga ol su isseoyo?* 언제 의사가 올 수 있어요?
Could I make an appointment to see the doctor?	*Jillyo yeyageul hal su isseul kkayo?* 진료예약을 할 수 있을까요?
I've got an appointment to see the doctor at...o'clock.	*...si e jillyo yeyageul haesseoyo.* ...시에 진료예약을 했어요.
Which doctor/pharmacy is on night/ weekend duty?	*Eoneu uisaga/yak gugi bame/ jumare ilhaeyo?* 어느 의사가/약국이 밤에/주말에 일해요?

13.2 What's wrong?

I don't feel well.	*Momi an joayo.* 몸이 안 좋아요.
I'm dizzy.	*Eojireo woyo.* 어지러워요.
I'm sick.	*Apayo.* 아파요.
I feel nauseous.	*Meseukkeo woyo.* 메스꺼워요.
I've got a cold.	*Gamgie geollyeo sseoyo.* 감기에 걸렸어요.
It hurts here.	*Yeogiga apayo.* 여기가 아파요.
I vomited.	*Tohae sseoyo.* 토했어요.
I've got …	*…i/ga isseoyo* …이/가 있어요
I'm running a temperature of…degrees.	*Cheoni …dona dwaeyo.* 체온이 …도나 돼요.
I've been stung by …	*…e ssoyeo sseoyo* …에 쏘였어요
a wasp	*beol* 벌
an insect	*beolle* 벌레
a jellyfish	*haepari* 해파리
I've been bitten by…	*…e mullyeo sseoyo* …에 물렸어요
a dog	*gae* 개
a snake	*baem* 뱀
an animal	*dongmul* 동물

I've cut myself.	*Sangcheo reul nae sseoyo.*
	상처를 냈어요.
I've burned myself.	*Hwasang eul ibeo sseoyo.*
	화상을 입었어요.
I've grazed myself.	*Chalgwa sangeul ibeo sseoyo.*
	찰과상을 입었어요.
I've had a fall.	*Neomeo jyeo sseoyo.*
	넘어졌어요.
I've sprained my ankle.	*Balmo geul ppieo sseoyo.*
	발목을 삐었어요.

13.3 The consultation

어떤 문제인 것 같아요?	What seems to be the problem?
이런 증세가 얼마나 오래됐어요?	How long have you had these complaints?
전에 이런 문제가 있었어요?	Have you had this trouble before?
열이 있어요? 얼마나 높아요?	Do you have a temperature? What is it?
옷을 벗으세요.	Get undressed, please.
허리까지 벗으세요.	Strip to the waist, please.
저기에서 벗으시면 돼요.	You can undress there.
왼쪽/오른쪽 소매를 걷어 올려 주세요.	Roll up your left/right sleeve, please.
여기에 누우세요.	Lie down here, please.
이렇게 하면 아파요?	Does this hurt?
숨을 깊이 쉬세요.	Breathe deeply.
입을 벌리세요.	Open your mouth.

Patient's medical history

I'm a diabetic.	*Dangnyo byeongi isseoyo.*
	당뇨병이 있어요.
I have a heart condition.	*Sim jang jil hwa ni isseoyo.*
	심장질환이 있어요.

I'm asthmatic.	*Cheon sigi isseoyo.* 천식이 있어요.
I'm allergic to …	*…allereu giga isseoyo* …에 알레르기가 있어요
I'm …months pregnant.	*Imsin …gaewo rieyo.* 임신 …개월이에요.
I'm on a diet.	*Jigeum sigiyo ppeobeul hago isseoyo.* 지금 식이요법을 하고 있어요.
I'm on medication.	*Jigeum yageul meokgo isseoyo.* 지금 약을 먹고 있어요.
I've had a heart attack once before.	*Jeone hanbeon simjang mabi reul han jeogi isseoyo.* 전에 한번 심장마비를 한 적이 있어요.
I've had a(n) …operation.	*…susulreul han jeogi isseoyo.* …수술을 한 적이 있어요.
I've been ill recently.	*Choegeune apass eoyo.* 최근에 아팠어요.
I've got a stomach ulcer.	*Wigwe yangi isseoyo.* 위궤양이 있어요.
I've got my period.	*Saengni jungi eyo.* 생리 중이에요.
I have a previous injury on my...	*… e jeonei beun busangi isseoyo.* … 에 전에 입은 부상이 있어요.
ankle	*balmok* 발목
knee	*mureup* 무릎
wrist	*sonmok* 손목

알레르기가 있어요?	Do you have any allergies?
지금 약을 복용 중이신가요?	Are you on any medication?
지금 식이요법 중이신가요?	Are you on a diet?
임신 중이신가요?	Are you pregnant?
파상풍 주사를 맞으신 적이 있나요?	Have you had a tetanus injection?

The diagnosis

심각한 건 아니에요.	It's nothing serious.
...이/가 부러졌네요	Your ... is broken
...삐었군요	You've got a sprained ...
...이/가 찢어졌군요	You've got a torn ...
염증이 있군요.	You've got some inflammation.
맹장염이군요.	You've got appendicitis.
기관지염이군요.	You've got bronchitis.
성병이군요.	You've got a venereal disease.
독감이군요.	You've got the flu.
심장마비이군요.	You've had a heart attack.
(바이러스성/박테리아성) 염증이에요.	You've got a (viral/ bacterial) infection.
폐렴이에요.	You've got pneumonia.
위염/위궤양이에요.	You've got gastritis/an ulcer.
근육이 늘어났군요.	You've pulled a muscle.
질염이군요.	You've got a vaginal infection.
식중독이에요.	You've got food poisoning.
일사병이에요.	You've got sunstroke.
...에 알레르기가 있군요	You're allergic to ...
임신이군요.	You're pregnant.
피/소변/대변 검사를 해야겠어요.	I'd like to have your blood/ urine/stools tested.
봉합 수술이 필요해요.	It needs stitches.
전문의한테 보내드리겠어요.	I'm referring you to a specialist.
엑스레이를 찍어야겠어요.	You'll need some x-rays taken.
수술을 해야겠어요.	You'll need an operation.
대기실에서 좀 기다려 주시겠어요?	Could you wait in the waiting room, please?

| Is it contagious? | *Igeo jeonyeom dwaeyo?* 이거 전염돼요? |
| How long do I have to stay ...? | *Eolmana orae ...isseoya dwaeyo?* 얼마나 오래 ...있어야 돼요? |

135

in bed	*nuwo* 누워
in the hospital	*byeong wone* 병원에
Do I have to go on a special diet?	*Sigiyo beobeul haeya dwaeyo?* 식이요법을 해야 돼요?
Am I allowed to travel?	*Yeohaeng eul haedo dwaeyo?* 여행을 해도 돼요?
Can I make another appointment?	*Daeum yeyageul hal su isseoyo?* 다음 예약을 할 수 있어요?
When do I have to come back?	*Eonje dasi waya dwaeyo?* 언제 다시 와야 돼요?
I'll come back tomorrow.	*Naeil dasi o gesseoyo.* 내일 다시 오겠어요.
How do I take this medicine?	*I yak eotteoke meogeoyo?* 이 약 어떻게 먹어요?

내일/...일 후에 다시 오세요	Come back tomorrow/in ...days' time

13.4 Medications and prescriptions

How many pills/drops/ spoonfuls/tablets each time?	*Han beone myeot al/bangul/seupun/ alssi gieyo?* 한 번에 몇 알/방울/스푼/알씩이에요?
How many times a day?	*Haru e myeot beon ssigiyo?* 하루에 몇 번씩이요?
I've forgotten to take my medication.	*Yak meongneun geoseul ijeo beoryeo sseoyo.* 약 먹는 것을 잊어버렸어요.
Could you write a prescription for me, please?	*Cheobangjeon jom sseo jusige sseoyo?* 처방전 좀 써 주시겠어요?

항생제/감기 물약/진정제/
진통제 처방 해드릴께요.
I'm prescribing antibiotics/a cough
 mixture/a tranquilizer/pain killers.

푹 쉬세요.
Gets lots of rest.

집에 계세요.
Stay indoors.

누워 계세요.
Stay in bed.

---

capsules
kaebsyul
캡슐

dissolve in water
mule nog iseyo
물에 녹이세요

swallow (whole)
(tong jjaelo) samki seyo
(통째로) 삼키세요

pills/tablets
alyag
알약

rub on
golu baleu seyo
고루 바르세요

External use only
oeyong
외용

drops
jeomgeog aeg
점적약

...for ...days
...il dongan
..일 동안

This medication impairs
 your driving.
*I yageun unjeonei jangae
 leul gajyeo omnida.*
이 약은 운전에 장애를
 가져옵니다.

injections
jusa
주사

before meals
sigjeone
식전에

ointment
yeongo
연고

every ...hours
mae ...sigan mada
매 ...시간마다

Finish the prescription.
*Cheobangjeon yageul
 kkeutkkaji deuseyo.*
처방전 약을 끝까지 드세요.

take
deuseyo
드세요

...times a day
halu e ...beonssig
하루에 ...번씩

spoonful/teaspoonful
han sudgal/han chas sudgal
한 숟갈/한 찻숟갈

13.5 At the dentist

Do you know a
 good dentist?
Jal haneun chikkwa uisa aseyo?
잘 하는 치과 의사 아세요?

Could you make a dental
 appointment for me?
Chikkwae yeyak jom hae jusi gesseoyo?
치과에 예약 좀 해 주시겠어요?

It's urgent.   *Geupaeyo.*
급해요.

Can I come in
today, please?   *Oneul gado dwaeyo?*
오늘 가도 돼요?

I have a
(terrible) toothache.   *Iga (simhage) apayo.*
이가 (심하게) 아파요.

Could you prescribe/
give me a painkiller?   *Jitongje jom cheobang hae jusige sseoyo?*
진통제 좀 처방해 주시겠어요?

I've got a broken tooth.   *Iga bureo jyeo sseoyo.*
이가 부러졌어요.

My filling's come out.   *I tteun ge ppajyeo sseoyo.*
이 떼운 게 빠졌어요.

I've got a broken crown.   *I sswiun ge manggajyeo sseoyo.*
이 씌운 게 망가졌어요.

I'd like/I don't want a
local anaesthetic.   *Gukbu machwi reul hae juseyo/haji maseyo.*
국부 마취를 해 주세요/하지 마세요.

Could you do a
temporary repair?   *Imsicheo bangeul jom haejusi gesseoyo?*
임시처방을 좀 해 주시겠어요?

I don't want this
tooth pulled.   *I ireul ppaego sipji anayo.*
이 이를 빼고 싶지 않아요.

My denture is broken.   *Teulliga manggajyeo sseoyo.*
틀니가 망가졌어요.

Can you fix it?   *Gochil su isseoyo?*
고칠 수 있어요?

Do I have to come back
to remove the stitches?   *Shileul bbopgi wihae dola waya haeyo?*
실을 뽑기 위해 돌아와야 해요?

When should I come back
to remove the stitches?   *Shilbap eonje puleoyo?*
실밥 언제 풀어요?

It hurts a lot/it's
very painful!   *Cham apayo!*
참 아파요!

어느 이가 아프세요?	Which tooth hurts?
고름이 생겼어요.	You've got an abscess.
근관치료를 해야겠어요.	I'll have to do a root canal.
국부 마취를 해야겠어요.	I'm giving you a local anaesthetic.
이 이를 뽑아야/떼워야/갈아야 되겠어요.	I'll have to pull/fill/file this tooth.
드릴을 해야겠어요.	I'll have to drill it.
입을 크게 벌리세요.	Open wide, please.
입을 다무세요.	Close your mouth, please.
입을 헹구세요.	Rinse, please.
아직도 아프세요?	Does it hurt still?

14. Emergencies

14.1 Asking for help
14.2 Lost items
14.3 Accidents
14.4 Theft
14.5 Missing person
14.6 The police

In an emergency, call 112 for the police and 119 for the fire or ambulance service. Many police boxes are located on the major streets of most cities. Alternatively, you can call the International SOS Korea (Tel: 82 (2) 3140 1700) for 24-hour emergency service assistance in English. For lost property, contact the Lost and Found Center of the Seoul Metropolitan Police Agency (Tel: 82-1566-0112).

14.1 Asking for help

Help!	*Dowa juseyo!* 도와 주세요!
Fire!	*Buri nasseoyo!* 불이 났어요!
Police!	*Gyeongcharyo!* 경찰요!
Quick/Hurry!	*Ppalliyo!* 빨리요!
Danger!	*Wiheom haeyo!* 위험해요!
Watch out!/Be careful!	*Josim haseyo!* 조심하세요!
Stop!	*Meomchu seyo!* 멈추세요!
Get your hands off me!	*Son chiwoyo!* 손 치워요!
Stop thief!	*Dodu giya!* 도둑이야!

Could you help me, please?	*Jeo jom dowa jusi gesseoyo?* 저 좀 도와 주시겠어요?
Where's the police emergency exit/ fire escape?	*Gyeongchalseo/bisang gu/bisang guga eodi e isseoyo?* 경찰서/비상구/비상구가 어디에 있어요?
Where's the nearest fire extinguisher?	*Sohwa giga eodi e isseoyo?* 소화기가 어디에 있어요?
Call the fire department!	*Sobang seo e yeollak haseyo!* 소방서에 연락하세요!
Call the police!	*Gyeongchale yeollak haseyo!* 경찰에 연락하세요!
Call an ambulance!	*Ambyulleon seureul bureu seyo!* 앰뷸런스를 부르세요!
Where's the nearest phone?	*Jenhwaga eodi e isseoyo?* 전화가 어디에 있어요?
Could I use your phone?	*Jeonhwa jom sseodo dwaeyo?* 전화 좀 써도 돼요?
What's the emergency number?	*Eunggeup jeonhwaga myeot beoni eyo?* 응급 전화가 몇 번이에요?
What's the number for the police?	*Gyeongchal jeonhwaga myeot beoni eyo?* 경찰 전화가 몇 번이에요?
I've lost my wallet/purse.	*Jiga beul ireo beoryeo sseoyo.* 지갑을 잃어버렸어요.

14.2 Lost items

I lost my …here yesterday.	*Eoje yeogiseo …eul/reul ireo beoryeo sseoyo.* 어제 여기서 …을/를 잃어버렸어요.
I left my …here.	*Yeogi e …eul/reul dueo sseoyo.* 여기에 …을/를 두었어요.
Did you find my…?	*Je … cha jasseoyo?* 제 … 찾았어요?
It was right here.	*Baro yeogi e isseo sseoyo.* 바로 여기에 있었어요.

It's very valuable.	*Aju sojunghan geoyeyo.* 아주 소중한 거예요.
Where's the lost and found office?	*Bunsil mulsen teoga eodi e isseoyo?* 분실물센터가 어디에 있어요?
I left it here/at the train station/on the train.	*Yeogi e/gicha yeoke/gichae ileo beolyeoss eoyo.* 여기에/기차역에/기차에 잃어버렸 어요.

14.3 Accidents

There's been an accident.	*Sagoga nasseoyo.* 사고가 났어요.
Someone's fallen into the water.	*Nuga mure ppajyeo sseoyo.* 누가 물에 빠졌어요.
There's a fire.	*Buri nasseoyo.* 불이 났어요.
Is anyone hurt?	*Dachin saram isseoyo?* 다친 사람 있어요?
Nobody has been injured.	*Amudo an dachyeo sseoyo.* 아무도 안 다쳤어요.
Someone has been injured.	*Nuga dachyeo sseoyo.* 누가 다쳤어요.
Someone's still trapped inside the car/train.	*Nuga ajikdo cha/gicha ane gatchyeo isseoyo.* 누가 아직도 차/기차 안에 갇혀 있어요.
It's not too bad.	*Aju nappeujin anayo.* 아주 나쁘지 않아요.
Don't worry.	*Geokjeong haji maseyo.* 걱정하지 마세요.
Leave everything the way it is, please.	*Inneun geudaero duseyo.* 있는 그대로 두세요.
I want to talk to the police first.	*Meonjeo gyeongchare singohae yagess eoyo.* 먼저 경찰에 신고해 야겠어요.
I want to take a photo first.	*Meonjeo sajineul jjigeoya gesseoyo.* 먼저 사진을 찍어야겠어요.

May I have your name and address?	*Seonghamgwa juso jom jusi gesseoyo?* 성함과 주소 좀 주시겠어요?
Here's my name and address.	*Yeogi je ireumgwa jusoga isseoyo.* 여기 제 이름과 주소가 있어요.
Could I see your identity card/ your insurance papers?	*Sinbunjeung/boheom jeung jom boyeo jusi gesseoyo?* 신분증/보험증 좀 보여 주시겠어요?
Would you act as a witness?	*Jeungini jom dwae jusi gesseoyo?* 증인이 좀 돼 주시겠어요?
I need this information for insurance purposes.	*Boheom cheonggu e i naeyongi piryo haeyo.* 보험 청구에 이 내용이 필요해요.
Are you insured?	*Boheom deureo sseoyo?* 보험 들었어요?
Third party or all inclusive?	*Samja daemul boheom ani myeon jonghap boheo mieyo?* 삼자 대물 보험 아니면 종합 보험이에요?
Could you sign here, please?	*Yeogi sa in jom hae jusi gesseoyo?* 여기 사인 좀 해 주시겠어요?

14.4 Theft

I've been robbed.	*Doduk eul majass eoyo.* 도둑을 맞았어요.
My... has been stolen.	*...eul/reul dodukeul majass eoyo.* ...을/를 도둑을 맞았어요.
My car's been broken into.	*Je cha e dodugi deureo sseoyo.* 제 차에 도둑이 들었어요.

14.5 Missing person

| I've lost my child/ grandmother. | *Uri ae/halmeoni ga eopseo jyeosseoyo.*
우리 애/할머니가 없어졌어요. |
| Could you help me find him/her? | *Jom chaja jusi gesseoyo?*
좀 찾아주시겠어요? |

Have you seen a small child?	*Eorin aireul mot bosyeoss nayo?* 어린 아이를 못 보셨나요?
He's/She's …years old	*Na ineun …sari eyo* 나이는 …살이에요
He/She's got …hair	*…meori yeyo* …머리예요
short/long	*jjalbeun/gin* 짧은/긴
blond/red/brown/ black/grey	*geumbal/ppalgansaek/galsaek/ geomeunsaek/hoesaek* 금발/빨간색/갈색/검은색/회색
curly/straight/frizzy	*weibeuga inneun/ilja/gopseul gopseul han* 웨이브가 있는/일자/곱슬곱슬한
in a ponytail/braids/bun	*dwiro mukkeun/ttaeun/dwiro ollin* 뒤로 묶은/땋은/ 뒤로 올린
He's/She's got blue/ brown/green eyes.	*Nuneun paransaek/galsek/ pureunsaek nuni eyo.* 눈은 파란색/갈색/푸른색 눈이에요.
He's/She's wearing swimming trunks/ a swimsuit.	*Banbaji suyeong bogeul ipgo isseoyo.* 반바지 수영복을 입고 있어요.
He's/She's wearing hiking boots.	*Deungsan hwareul sinkko isseoyo.* 등산화를 신고 있어요.
with/without glasses	*angyeong eul kkigo/an kkigo* 안경을 끼고/안 끼고
carrying/not carrying a bag	*gabangeul deulgo/an deulgo* 가방을 들고/안 들고
He/She is tall/short.	*Kiga keoyo/jagayo.* 키가 커요/작아요.
This is a photo of him/her.	*Ige geu ae saji nieyo.* 이게 그 애 사진이에요.
He/she must be lost.	*Teulli meopsi gireul ireo sseoyo.* 틀림없이 길을 잃었어요.

14.6 The police

An arrest

면허증 좀 보여 주세요.	Your driver's license, please.
속도위반입니다.	You were speeding.
여기 주차하시면 안 됩니다.	You're not allowed to park here.
주차비를 안 내셨습니다.	You haven't paid the parking fee.
라이트가 안 들어옵니다.	Your lights aren't working.
... 원 벌금입니다	That's a ... won fine.
지금 내시겠습니까?	Do you want to pay now?
지금 내셔야 합니다.	You'll have to pay now.
어디서 일어났습니까?	Where did it happen?
뭐가 없어졌습니까?	What's missing?
뭘 가져갔습니까?	What's been taken?
신분증 좀 보여 주시겠습니까?	Could I see your identity card/ some identification?
그게 몇 시였습니까?	What time did it happen?
증인이 있습니까?	Are there any witnesses?
여기 서명하세요.	Sign here, please.
통역이 필요하십니까?	Do you want an interpreter?

I don't speak Korean.	*Hanggungmal mot hamnida.* 한국말 못 합니다.
I didn't see the sign.	*Pyoji paneul mot bwasseoyo.* 표지판을 못 봤어요.
I don't understand what it says.	*Museun marinji moreu geosseoyo.* 무슨 말인지 모르겠어요.
I was only doing ... kilometers an hour.	*Danji ... kiroyeon neundeyo.* 시속 ... 키로였는데요.
I'll have my car checked.	*Cha jeongni reul matgi geosseoyo.* 차 정비를 맡기겠어요.
I was blinded by oncoming lights.	*Majeun pyeon charyang bulbit ttaemune bol suga eopsseo sseoyo.* 맞은편 차량 불빛 때문에 볼 수가 없었어요.

At the police station

I want to report a collision/missing person/rape.	*Chungdol sago reul/siljjong sakkeu neul/ganggan sakkeo neul singoha gosip eoyo.* 충돌 사고를/실종 사건을/강간 사건을 신고하 고싶어요.
Could you make a statement, please?	*Jinsul seoreul jom sseo jusi gesseoyo?* 진술서를 좀 써 주시겠어요?
Could I have a copy for the insurance?	*Boheom yongeuro sabon han jang jom jusi gesseoyo?* 보험용으로 사본 한 장 좀 주시겠어요?
I've lost everything.	*Da ireo beoryeo sseoyo.* 다 잃어버렸어요.
I've no money left.	*Doni hanado eopseoyo.* 돈이 하나도 없어요.
Could you lend me a little money?	*Doneul jogeum billyeo jusi gesseoyo?* 돈을 조금 빌려 주시겠어요?
I'd like an interpreter.	*Tong yeogi piryo haeyo.* 통역이 필요해요.
I'm innocent.	*Jeneun joega eopseoyo.* 저는 죄가 없어요.
I don't know anything about it.	*Geu e daehae seo amu geotdo moreum nida.* 그에 대해서 아무것도 모릅니다.
I want to speak to someone from the... embassy	*Daesagwan jigwongwa yaegi hago sipeoyo* ... 대사관 직원과 얘기하고 싶어요 ...
American	*Miguk* 미국
British	*Yeongguk* 영국
Canadian	*Kaenada* 캐나다
I want a lawyer who speaks English.	*Yeongeoreul haneun byeonho sareul bulleo juseyo.* 영어를 하는 변호사를 불러 주세요.

Okay. I'm prescribing some medicine.
Jota, yakcheobang halkkeyo?

Do I have to go on a special diet?
Sigiyo beobeul haeya dwaeyo?

Yes, doctor. Thank you.
Ye, uisa. Gamsa hamnida.

Yes, avoid eating oily foods. Try to drink more fluids. Take these pills three times a day.
Gileunjin eunsig eulpi. Deoman heun eumnyo reul mashiseyo. Iyag eul 3 baehalue geolli seyo.

15. English-Korean Dictionary

This dictionary is meant to supplement the previous chapters. Some of the words not on this list can be found elsewhere in this book. Food items can be found in Section 4.7, the parts of the car on page 65, the parts of a bicycle on page 69 and camping/backpacking equipment on page 90.

A

about, approximately	...정도	...jeongdo
about, regarding	...에 대해	...e daehae
above, upstairs	...위에	...wi e
abroad	해외에(서)	haeoe e(seo)
accident	사고	sago
adaptor	어댑터	eodaepteo
address	주소	juso
admission	입장	ipjang
admission price	입장료	ipjang nyo
adult	어른	eoreun
advice	충고	chunggo
aeroplane	비행기	bihaenggi
after (place)	뒤에	...dwi e
after (time)	후에	...hu e
afternoon	오후	ohu
aftershave	애프터 쉐이브	aepeuteo sweibeu
again	다시	dasi
age	나이	na i
AIDS	에이즈	E i jeu
air conditioning	냉난방	naeng nanbang
air mattress	공기 매트리스	gonggi maeteu riseu
airmail	항공 우편	hanggong upyeon
airplane	비행기	bihaenggi
airport	공항	gonghang
alarm (emergency)	경보	gyeongbo
alarm clock	알람 시계	allam sigye
alcohol, liquor	술	sul
all day	종일	jongil
all the time	항상	hangsang
allergy	알레르기	alle reugi
alone	혼자 있다, 혼자(서)	honja itda, honja (seo)
altogether, in total	모두	modu
always	항상	hangsang
ambassador	대사	daesa
ambulance	앰뷸런스	aembyul leonseu
America	미국	Miguk
American	미국 사람	Miguk saram
amount	양, 금액	yang, geumaek

amusement park	놀이 공원	nori gongwon
anesthetic (general)	전신 마취	jeonsin machwi
anesthetic (local)	국부 마취	gukbu machwi
angry	화나다, 화난	hwanada, hwanan
animal	동물	dongmul
ankle	발목	balmok
answer the phone, to	전화 받다	jeonhwa batda
answer, respond (written), to	답장하다	dapjang hada
answer, respond, to	대답하다	daedap hada
answer, response (spoken)	대답	daedap
answer, response (written)	답장	dapjang
answering machine	자동 응답기	jadong eungdapgi
ant	개미	gaemi
antibiotics	항생제	hangsaengje
antifreeze	부동액	budongaek
antiques	골동품	golttongpum
antiseptic	소독약	sodongyak
anus	항문	hangmun
anybody, anyone	누구든지	nugu deunji
anything	무엇이든지	mueosi deunji
anywhere	어디든지	eodi deunji
apartment	아파트	apateu
apologise, to	사과하다	sagwa hada
apple	사과	sagwa
apple juice	사과주스	sagwa juseu
apply (for permission), to	신청하다	sincheong hada
appointment	약속, 임명	yaksok, immyeong
April	사월	Sawol
architecture	건축	geonchuk
area	지역	jiyeok
area code	지역 번호	jiyeok beonho
arm	팔	pal
arrange, to	준비하다	junbi hada
arrival	도착	dochak
arrive, to	도착하다	dochak hada
arrow	화살	hwasal
art	예술	yesul
art gallery	미술관	misul gwan
artery	동맥	dongmaek
article (in newspaper)	기사	gisa
ashtray	재떨이	jaetteori
ask, to	물어보다	mureo boda
ask for, request, to	부탁하다	butak hada
aspirin	아스피린	aseu pirin
assault	폭행	pokhaeng
assorted	종합한	jonghaphan
at home	집에	jibe
at night	밤에	bame
at the back	뒤에	dwi e
at the front	앞에	a pe
at the latest, no later than	늦어도	neujeodo
attractive	매력적이다/-적인	maeryeok jeogida, maeryeok jeogin

English	Korean	Romanization
aubergine, eggplant	가지	gaji
August	팔월	Parwol
Australia	호주	Hoju
Australian	호주 사람	Hoju saram
automatic	자동	jadong
autumn	가을	ga eul
awake	깨어 있는	kkae eo ineun
awning	차양	cha yang

B

English	Korean	Romanization
baby	아기	agi
baby food	이유식	iyusik
babysitter	보모	bomo
back (part of body)	등	deung
back, rear	뒤	dwi
backpack	배낭	baenang
backpacker	배낭 여행자	baenang yeohaengja
backward	뒤로	dwiro
bad (rotting)	상하다, 상한	sanghada, sanghan
bad (terrible)	나쁘다, 나쁜	nappeuda, nappeun
bag	가방	gabang
bakery	빵집	ppangjjip
balcony	발코니	balkoni
ball	공	gong
ball point pen	볼펜	bolpen
banana	바나나	banana
bandage	붕대	bungdae
bandaids	일회용 반창고	ilhoeyong banchanggo
bangs, fringe	앞머리	ammeori
bank (finance)	은행	eunhaeng
bank (river)	둑	duk
bar (café)	카페	kape
barbecue	바베큐	babekyu
bargain, to	흥정하다	heungjeong hada
baseball	야구	yagu
basketball	농구	nonggu
bath	목욕	mogyok
bath towel	목욕 타월	mogyok tawol
bath mat	목욕탕 매트	mogyok tang maeteu
bathrobe	목욕 가운	mogyok gaun
bathroom	화장실, 목욕실	hwajangsil, mogyoksil
battery	배터리, 건전지	baeteori, geonjeonji
beach	바닷가	badatga
beans	콩	kong
beautiful (of people)	예쁘다, 예쁜	yeppeuda, yeppeun
beautiful (of places)	아름답다/-다운	areum dapda, areum daun
beautiful (of things)	멋지다, 멋진	meotjida, meotjin
because	-기 때문에	-gi ttaemune
become, to	되다	doeda
bed	침대	chimdae
bedding, bedclothes	침구	chimgu
bee	벌	beol

beef	쇠고기	*soegogi*
beer	맥주	*maekju*
before (in front of)	앞에	*a pe*
before (in time)	전에	*jeone*
begin, to	시작하다	*sijak hada*
behind	뒤에	*dwi e*
below, downstairs	아래에	*are e*
belt	벨트	*belteu*
berth	침대	*chimdae*
beside	옆에	*yeope*
better, get (improve), to	좋아지다	*joa jida*
between	…사이에	*…sa ie*
bicycle	자전거	*jajeon geo*
big	크다, 큰	*keuda, keun*
bikini	비키니	*bikini*
bill	계산서	*gyesanseo*
billiards	당구	*danggu*
birthday	생일	*saengil*
biscuit	비스켓, 과자	*biseuket, gwaja*
bite, to	물다	*mulda*
bitter	쓰다, 쓴	*sseuda, sseun*
black	까맣다, 까만	*kkamata, kkaman*
black and white	흑백	*heukbaek*
black eye	멍든 눈	*meongdeun nun*
bland (taste)	무미하다/-한	*mumi hada/-han*
blanket	담요	*damyo*
bleach, to	탈색하다	*talsaek hada*
bleed, to	피를 흘리다	*pireul heullida*
blind (unable to see)	눈이 멀다, 눈먼	*nuni meolda, nunmeon*
blind (on window)	블라인드	*beulla indeu*
blister	물집	*muljjip*
blog	블로그	*beullogeu*
blond	금발	*geumbal*
blood	피	*pi*
blood pressure	혈압	*hyeorap*
bloody nose, to have	코피가 나다	*kopiga nada*
blouse	블라우스	*beulla useu*
blue	파랗다, 파란	*parata, paran*
boat	배	*bae*
body	몸	*mom*
boiled	끓인, 삶은	*kkeurin, salmeun*
bone	뼈	*ppyeo*
book	책	*chaek*
booked, reserved	예약되다, 예약된	*yeyak doeda, yeyak doen*
booking office	예매소	*yemaeso*
bookshop	서점	*seojeom*
border, edge	가장자리	*gajang jari*
bored	심심하다	*simsim hada*
boring	지루하다, 지루한	*jiru hada, jiruhan*
born, to be	태어나다	*tae eo nada*
borrow, to	빌리다	*billida*
botanic gardens	식물원	*singmurwon*
both	둘 다	*dul da*

English	Korean	Romanization
bottle (baby's)	젖병	jeotbyeong
bottle (wine)	술병	sulppyeong
bottle-warmer	젖병 보온기	jeotbyeong bo ongi
box	상자	sangja
box office	매표소	maepyoso
boy	소년	sonyeon
boyfriend	남자 친구	namja chingu
bra	브라	beura
bracelet	팔찌	paljji
brake	브레이크	beure ikeu
brake oil	브레이크 오일	beure ikeu oil
bread	빵	ppang
break, shatter, to	깨뜨리다	kkaetteu rida
breakfast, morning meal	아침 식사	achim siksa
breast milk	모유	moyu
breasts	가슴	gaseum
bridge	다리	dari
briefs	팬티	paenti
bring, to	가져오다	gajyeo oda
brochure	브로셔	beurosyeo
broken (of bones, etc.)	부러지다, 부러진	bureo jida, bureo jin
broken (does not work)	고장나다/-난	gojang nada, gojang nan
bronze	청동	cheongdong
broth, soup	국	guk
brother	형제	hyeongje
brown	갈색(의)	galsaek(ui)
bruise	멍	meong
brush	솔, 붓	sol, but
bucket	양동이	yangdongi
Buddhism	불교	Bulgyo
buffet	뷔페	bwipe
bugs	벌레	beolle
building	빌딩	bilding
bun	롤빵	rolppang
burglary	도난, 강도	donan, gangdo
burn (injury)	화상	hwasang
burn, to	태우다, 타다	tae uda, tada
bus	버스	beoseu
bus station	버스 정거장	beoseu jeong geojang
bus stop	버스 정류장	beoseu jeong nyujang
business card	명함	myeongham
business class	비지니스 클라스	biji niseu keullaseu
business trip	출장	chuljang
busy (schedule)	바쁘다, 바쁜	bappeu da, bappeun
busy (traffic)	복잡하다, 복잡한	bokjap hada, bokja pan
but	그러나, -지만	geureona, -jiman
butane	부탄가스	butan gaseu
butchers	정육점	jeongyukjeom
butter	버터	beoteo
button	단추	danchu
buy, to	사다	sada
by airmail	항공우편으로	hanggong upyeo neuro
by phone	전화로	jeonhwaro

C

cabbage	양배추	*yangbaechu*
cabbage, Chinese	배추	*baechu*
cabin (boat)	선실	*seonsil*
cake, pastry	케이크	*ke ikeu*
call (phone call)	전화	*jeonhwa*
call, phone, to	전화하다	*jeonhwa hada*
called, named	불리다, 불리는	*bullida, bulli neun*
camera	카메라	*kamera*
camera memory	카메라 메모리	*kamera memori*
camping	캠핑	*kaemping*
can opener	깡통 따개	*kkangtong ttagae*
can, be able to	-(으)ㄹ 수 있다	*-(eu)l su itda*
can, may	-아/어도 좋다/되다	*-a/eodo jota/doeda*
cancel, to	취소하다	*chwiso hada*
candle	양초	*yangcho*
candy, sweets	사탕	*satang*
cap	모자	*moja*
capable of, to be	-(으)ㄹ 수 있다	*-(eu)l su itda*
car, automobile	자동차	*jadongcha*
car documents	차량 등록증	*charyang deungnokjeung*
car seat (child's)	어린이 보호 좌석	*eorini boho jwaseok*
car trouble	차량 고장	*charyang gojang*
cardigan	카디간	*kadigan*
Careful!	조심하세요!	*Josim haseyo!*
carpet	카페트	*kapeteu*
carriage, pram	유모차	*yumocha*
carrot	당근	*danggeun*
cartridge	카트릿지	*kateuritji*
cash, money	현금	*hyeongeum*
cash card	현금 카드	*hyeongeum kadeu*
cash desk	계산대	*gyesan dae*
cash machine	현금 지급기	*hyeongeum jigeupgi*
casino	카지노	*kajino*
cat	고양이	*goyangi*
catalogue	카탈로그	*katal logeu*
cauliflower	컬리플라워	*keollipeul lawo*
cause	원인	*wonin*
cave	동굴	*donggul*
CD	씨디	*Ssi Di*
CD-ROM	씨디-롬	*Ssi Di Rom*
celebrate, to	축하하다	*chukha hada*
cemetery	공동묘지	*gongdong myoji*
centimetre	센티미터	*senti miteo*
central heating	중앙 난방	*jungang nanbang*
central locking	중앙 잠금 장치	*jungang janggeum jangchi*
center (middle)	중앙, 가운데	*jungang, ga unde*
center (of city)	(시내) 중심지	*(sinae) jungsimji*
certificate	증명서	*jeung myeongseo*
chair	의자	*uija*
chambermaid	메이드	*meideu*
champagne	샴페인	*syampein*

change (money)	잔돈	*jandon*
change (trains)	바꿔타다	*bakkwo tada*
change the baby's diaper	기저귀를 갈다	*gijeo gwireul galda*
change the oil	오일을 갈다	*o ireul galda*
change, exchange (money), to	환전하다	*hwanjeon hada*
change, swap, to	바꾸다	*bakkuda*
charter flight	전세기 편	*jeonsegi pyeon*
chat, to	이야기하다	*iyagi hada*
cheap	싸다, 싼	*ssada, ssan*
check in	체크인하다	*chekeu in hada*
check out	체크아웃하다	*chekeu aut hada*
check, cheque	수표	*supyo*
check, verify, to	체크하다	*chekeu hada*
checked luggage	체크한 여행가방	*chekeu han yeohaeng gabang*
Cheers!	건배!	*Geonbae!*
cheese	치즈	*chijeu*
chef	요리사	*yorisa*
chess	체스	*cheseu*
chewing gum	껌	*kkeom*
chicken	닭(고기)	*dak(gogi)*
child	아이/애, 어린이	*a i/ae, eorini*
child's seat (in car)	어린이 보호 좌석	*eorini boho jwaseok*
chili paste	고추장	*gochujang*
chin	턱	*teok*
China	중국	*Jungguk*
chocolate	초콜렛	*chokollet*
choose, to	선택하다	*seontaek hada*
chopsticks	젓가락	*jeot garak*
Christianity	기독교	*Gidokgyo*
church	교회	*gyohoe*
church service	예배	*yebae*
cigar	시가	*siga*
cigarette	담배	*dambae*
cinema	극장	*geukjang*
circus	서커스	*seokeoseu*
citizen	시민	*simin*
city	도시	*dosi*
clean	깨끗하다, 깨끗한	*kkaekkeut hada, kkaekeutan*
clean, to	청소하다	*cheongso hada*
clearance (sale)	세일	*seil*
climate	기후	*gihu*
clock	시계	*sigye*
closed (shop)	끝나다, 끝난	*kkeun nada, kkeunnan*
closed off (road)	(도로가) 차단되다	*(do ro ga) chadan doeda*
cloth	옷감	*otgam*
clothes dryer	건조기	*geon jogi*
clothes hanger	옷걸이	*otgeori*
clothes, clothing	옷	*ot*
cloudy, overcast	흐리다, 흐린	*heurida, heurin*
clutch (car)	클러치	*keulleochi*
coat, overcoat	코트	*koteu*

15

cockroach	바퀴벌레	*bakwi beolle*
cocoa	코코아	*kokoa*
coffee	커피	*keopi*
coin	동전	*dongjeon*
cold (not hot)	춥다, 추운	*chupda, chu un*
cold, flu	감기	*gamgi*
collar	칼라	*kalla*
collarbone	쇄골	*swaegol*
colleague, co-worker	동료	*dongnyo*
collide, to	충돌하다	*chungdol hada*
collision	충돌	*chungdol*
cologne	화장수	*hwajangsu*
color	색	*saek*
comb	빗	*bit*
come, to	오다	*oda*
company, firm	회사	*hoesa*
compartment	칸	*kan*
complaint	불평	*bulpyeong*
completely	완전히	*wanjeonhi*
compliment	칭찬	*chingchan*
computer	컴퓨터	*keompyuteo*
computer game	컴퓨터 게임	*keompyuteo geim/ computer geim*
concert	콘서트	*konseoteu*
concert hall	콘서트 홀	*konseoteu hol*
concierge	수위	*suwi*
concussion	뇌진탕	*noejintang*
condensed milk	연유	*yeonyu*
condom	콘돔	*kondom*
confectionery	과자	*gwaja*
Congratulations!	축하해요!	*Chukha haeyo!*
connection (transport)	연결편	*yeongyeol pyeon*
constipation	변비	*byeonbi*
consulate	영사관	*yeongsagwan*
consultation (by doctor)	진찰	*jinchal*
contact lens	콘택트 렌즈	*kontaekteu renjeu*
contagious	전염되다, 전염되는	*jeonyeom doeda, jeonyeom doeneun*
contraceptive	피임	*pi im*
contraceptive pill	피임약	*pi imyak*
cook (person)	요리사	*yorisa*
cook, to	요리하다	*yori hada*
cookie, sweet biscuit	쿠키	*kuki*
copper	구리	*guri*
copy	사본, 복사	*sabon, boksa*
copy, to	복사하다	*boksa hada*
corkscrew	코르크 따개	*koreukeu ttagae*
corner	코너	*koneo*
cornflower	옥수수 가루	*oksusu garu*
correct, to	고치다	*gochida*
correspond (letters), to	편지 연락하다	*pyeonji yeollak hada*
corridor	복도	*bokdo*
cosmetics	화장품	*hwajangpum*

156

costume	의상	*uisang*
cotton	면	*myeon*
cotton wool	솜	*som*
cough	기침	*gichim*
cough syrup	기침 물약	*gichim mullyak*
cough, to	기침하다	*gichim hada*
counter (for paying, buying tickets)	카운트	*kaunteu*
country (nation)	나라	*nara*
country (rural area)	시골	*sigol*
country code	국가 번호	*gukga beonho*
courgettes, zucchini	(애)호박	*(ae)hobak*
course of treatment	치료	*chiryo*
cousin	사촌	*sachon*
crab	게	*ge*
cracker, salty biscuit	크래커	*keuraekeo*
cream	크림	*keurim*
credit card	신용카드	*sinyong kadeu*
cot, crib	아기 침대	*agi chimdae*
crime	범죄	*beomjoe*
crockery	그릇	*geureut*
cross, angry	화나다, 화난	*hwanada, hwa nan*
cross (road, river), to	건너다	*geonneoda*
crossroad	교차로	*gyocharo*
crosswalk, pedestrian crossing	건널목	*geonneol mok*
crutch	목발	*mokbal*
cry, to	울다	*ulda*
cubic metre	입방미터	*ipbang miteo*
cucumber	오이	*oi*
cuddly toy	동물 인형	*dongmul inhyeong*
cuffs	소매단	*somaedan*
cup	컵	*keop*
curly	곱슬하다/-한	*gopseul hada/-han*
current (electric)	전류	*jeollyu*
curtains	커튼	*keoteun*
cushion	쿠션	*kusyeon*
custom (tradition)	관습	*gwanseup*
customs	세관	*segwan*
cut (injury)	상처	*sangcheo*
cut, to	자르다	*jareda*
cutlery	포크, 나이프, 스푼	*pokeu, naipeu, seupun*
cycling	자전거 타기	*jajeongeo tagi*
Cyworld	싸이월드	*Ssaiwoldeu/Cyworld*

D

dairy products	유제품	*yujepum*
damage	손해, 손상	*sonhae, sonsang*
dance	춤	*chum*
dance, to	춤추다	*chumchuda*
dandruff	비듬	*bideum*
danger	위험	*wiheom*
dangerous	위험하다, 위험한	*wiheom hada, wiheom han*

dark	어둡다/진하다, 어두운/진한	eodupda/jinhada, eodu un/jinhan
date (of the month)	날짜	naljja
date of birth	생년월일	saengnyeon woril
daughter	딸	ttal
day	날, 낮	nal, nat
day after tomorrow	모레	mo re
day before yesterday	그저께	geujeokke
dead	죽다, 죽은	jukda, jugeun
deaf	귀가 먹다/먹은	gwiga meokda/meogeun
decaffeinated	카페인 없는	kapein eomneun
December	십이월	Sibiwol
declare (customs)	신고	singo
deep	깊다, 깊은	gipda, gipeun
deep freeze, freezer	냉동고	naengdonggo
deep-sea diving	스킨 다이빙	seukin daibing
defecate, to	배설하다	baeseol hada
degrees (temperature)	도	do
delay	지연	jiyeon
delete, to	삭제하다, 지우다	sakje hada, jiuda
delicious	맛있다, 맛있는	masitda, masin neun
dentist	치과(의사)	chikkwa(uisa)
dentures	틀니	teulli
deodorant	탈취제	talchwije
department store	백화점	baekhwajeom
departure	출발	chulbal
depilatory cream	탈모제	talmoje
deposit (for safekeeping), to	보관하다	bogwan hada
deposit (in the bank), to	예금하다	yegeum hada
desert (arid land)	사막	samak
dessert	디저트	dijeoteu
destination	목적지	mokjeokji
detergent	세제	seje
develop (film), to	현상하다	hyeonsang hada
diabetic	당뇨병 환자	dangnyobyeong hwanja
dial (telephone), to	전화하다	jeonhwa hada
diamond	다이아몬드	da i amondeu
diaper	기저귀	gojeogwi
diarrhea	설사	seolsa
dictionary	사전	sajeon
diesel oil	디젤유	di jellyu
diet	식이요법	sigi yobeop
difficulty	어려움	eo ryeo um
dining car	식당칸	sikdangkan
dining room	식당	sikdang
dinner, evening meal	저녁 식사	jeonyeok siksa
direct flight	직항	jikhang
direction	방향	banghyang
directly	직접	jikjeop
dirty	더럽다, 더러운	deoreopda, deoreo un
disabled person	장애인	jangaein
discount	디스카운트	diseuka unteu

discuss, to	의논하다	*uinon hada*
discussion	의논	*uinon*
dish (particular food)	요리	*yori*
dish of the day	오늘의 스페셜	*oneurui seupesyeol*
disinfectant	소독제	*sodokje*
dislike, to	싫어하다	*sireo hada*
distance	거리	*geori*
distilled water	증류수	*jeungnyusu*
disturb, to	방해하다	*banghae hada*
disturbance	방해	*banghae*
dive, to	다이빙하다	*daibing hada*
diving	다이빙	*daibing*
diving board	다이빙 보드	*daibing bodeu*
diving gear	다이빙 장비	*daibing jangbi*
divorced	이혼하다, 이혼한	*ihon hada, ihonhan*
dizzy	어지럽다, 어지러운	*eojireop da, eojireo un*
do not disturb	방해하지 마세요	*banghae haji maseyo*
do, perform an action, to	하다	*hada*
doctor	의사	*uisa*
dog	개	*gae*
doll	인형	*inhyeong*
domestic (flight)	국내선	*gungnae seon*
Don't!	그러지 마세요!	*Geureoji maseyo!*
done (cooked)	잘 익다, 잘 익은	*jal ikda, jal igeun*
door	문	*mun*
double	두 배	*du bae*
down, downward	아래로	*araero*
drapes, curtains	커튼	*keoteun*
dream, to	꿈꾸다	*kkumkkuda*
dress, frock	드레스	*deureseu*
dressing gown	실내복	*sillaebok*
dressing table	화장대	*hwajangdae*
drink (alcoholic)	술	*sul*
drink (refreshment)	음료(수)	*eumnyo(su)*
drink, to	마시다	*masida*
drinking water	식수	*siksu*
drive (a car), to	운전하다	*unjeon hada*
driver	운전사	*unjeon sa*
driver's license	운전 면허증	*unjeon myeonheojeung*
drugstore, pharmacy	약국	*yak guk*
drunk	술 취하다	*sul chwihada*
dry	마르다, 마른	*mareuda, mareun*
dry, to	말리다	*mallida*
dry-clean	드라이 클리닝	*deurai keullining*
dry cleaners	세탁소	*setakso*
duck	오리	*ori*
during, for	…동안	*…dongan*
duty (import tax)	관세	*gwanse*
duty-free goods	면세품	*myeonsepum*
duty-free shop	면세점	*myeonsejeom*
DVD	디비디	*Di Bi Di*

E

ear	귀	gwi
ear drops	귀 물약	gwi mullyak
earache	이통	itong
early	이르다, 이른	ireuda, ireun
earrings	귀걸이	gwigeori
earth, soil	흙	heuk
earthenware	도기	dogi
east	동쪽	dongjjok
easy	쉽다, 쉬운	swipda, swiun
eat, to	먹다	meokda
economy class	이코노미석	ikono miseok
eczema	습진	seupjin
eel	장어	jangeo
egg	계란, 알	gyeran, al
eggplant, aubergine	가지	gaji
electric	전기(의)	jeongi(ui)
electricity	전기	jeongi
electronic	전자(의)	jeonja(ui)
elephant	코끼리	kokkiri
elevator	엘리베이터	elli beiteo
email (message)	이메일	imeil
email address	이메일 주소	imeil juso
embassy	대사관	daesagwan
embroidery	(자)수	(ja)su
emergency	응급(사태)	eunggeup (satae)
emergency brake	비상 브레이크	bisang beure ikeu
emergency exit	비상구	bisanggu
emergency phone	응급 전화	eunggeup jeonhwa
emergency room	응급실	eunggeupsil
empty	텅 비다/빈	teong bida/bin
engaged (telephone)	통화중이다/-중인	tonghwa jungida/-jungin
engaged (to be married)	약혼하다/-한	yakon hada/-han
England	영국	Yeongguk
English	영어	Yeongeo
enjoy, to	즐기다	jeulgida
enquire, to	물어보다	mureo boda
envelope	봉투	bongtu
escalator	에스컬레이터	eseu keolle iteo
essential	필수적이다, 필수적인	pilsu jeogida, pilsu jeogin
evening	저녁	jeonyeok
evening wear	야회복	yahoebok
event	행사	haengsa
every	모든, 매…	modeun, mae…
everybody, everyone	모든 사람	modeun saram
everything	모든 것	modeun geot
everywhere	어디든지, 모든 곳	eodi deunji, modeun got
examine, to	검토하다, 진찰하다	geomto hada, jinchal hada
excavation	발굴	balgul
excellent	우수하다, 우수한	usu hada, usu han
exchange (money, opinions), to	교환하다	gyohwan hada
exchange office	환전소	hwanjeonso

English	Korean	Romanization
exchange rate	환율	*hwannyul*
Excuse me!	실례합니다!	*Sillye hamnida!*
Excuse me! (apology)	미안합니다!	*Mian hamnida!*
exhibition	전시회	*jeonsihoe*
exit, way out	출구	*chulgu*
expense	비용	*biyong*
expensive	비싸다, 비싼	*bissada, bissan*
explain, to	설명하다	*seolmyeong hada*
express, state, to	표현하다	*pyohyeon hada*
eye	눈	*nun*
eye drops	눈약	*nunyak*
eye specialist	안과 전문의	*ankkwa jeonmunui*

F

English	Korean	Romanization
fabric, textile	직물	*jingmul*
face	얼굴	*eolgul*
Facebook	페이스북	*Pei seubuk*
factory	공장	*gong ang*
fall (season)	가을	*ga eul*
fall over, to	넘어지다	*neomeo jida*
family	가족	*gajok*
famous	유명하다, 유명한	*yumyeong hada, yumyeong han*
fan (admirer)	팬	*paen*
fan (for cooling)	부채	*buchae*
far away	멀다, 먼	*meolda, meon*
farm	농장	*nongjang*
farmer	농부	*nongbu*
fashion	패션	*paesyeon*
fast, rapid	빠르다, 빠른	*ppareuda, ppareun*
father	아버지	*abeoji*
father-in-law	시아버지, 장인	*sia beoji, jangin*
fault	잘못	*jalmot*
fax	팩스	*paekseu*
fax, to	팩스 보내다	*paekseu bonaeda*
February	이월	*Iwol*
feel like	-고 싶다	*-go sipda*
feel, to	느끼다	*neukkida*
female	여성	*yeoseong*
fence	담, 울타리	*dam, ultari*
ferry	배	*bae*
fever	열	*yeol*
fiancé	약혼자	*yakonja*
fiancée	약혼녀	*yakonnyeo*
fill out (form), to	작성하다	*jakseong hada*
fill, to	채우다	*chae uda*
film (camera)	필름	*pilleum*
filter	필터	*pilteo*
fine (good)	좋다, 좋은	*jota, joeun*
fine (money)	벌금	*beolgeum*
finger	손가락	*sonkkarak*
fire	불	*bul*
fire alarm	화재 경보	*hwajae gyeongbo*

English	Korean	Romanization
fire department, fire service	소방서	sobangseo
fire escape	비상구	bisanggu
fire extinguisher	소화기	sohwagi
first	첫 번째	cheot beonjjae
first aid	응급 조치	eunggeup jochi
first class	일등석	ildeungseok
fish (live)	물고기	mulkkogi
fish (food)	생선	saengseon
fishing	낚시	naksi
fishing rod	낚싯대	naksitdae
fitness club	헬스 클럽	helseu keulleop
fitness training	체력 단련	cheryeok dallyeon
fitting room	탈의실	taruisil
fix (repair), to	고치다	gochida
flag	깃발	gitbal
flash (camera)	플래쉬	peullaeswi
flashlight, torch	손전등	sonjeondeung
flatulence	복부 팽만	bokbu paengman
flavor	맛	mat
flavoring	첨가물	cheomgamul
flea	벼룩	byeoruk
flea market	벼룩시장	byeoruk sijang
flight	운항	unhang
flight number	운항 번호	unhang beonho
flood	홍수	hongsu
floor	마루, 층	maru, cheung
flour	밀가루	milkkaru
flower	꽃	kkot
flu	독감	dokgam
flush (toilet), to	변기 물을 내리다	byeongi mureul naerida
fly (insect)	파리	pari
fly, to	날다	nalda
fog	안개	angae
foggy	안개끼다, 안개낀	angae kkida, angae kkin
folklore	민담	mindam
follow behind, to	뒤따라가다	dwitta ragada
food (meal)	음식	eumsik
food court	음식 백화점	eumsik baekhwajeom
food poisoning	식중독	sikjungdok
foot	발	bal
foot brake	발 브레이크	bal beure ikeu
forbidden	금지되다, 금지된	geumji doeda, geumji doen
forehead	이마	ima
foreign	외국(의)	oeguk(ui)
foreigner	외국인	oegugin
forget, to	잊어버리다	ijeobeo rida
fork	포크	pokeu
form (application)	신청서	sincheongseo
form (to fill out), to	작성하다	jakseong hada
formal dress	정장	jeongjang
fountain	분수	bunsu
frame (photo)	액자	aekja

free (no charge)	무료(의)	*muryo(ui)*
free (unoccupied)	비어있다, 비어있는	*bieo itda, bieo inneun*
free time	자유시간	*jayu sigan*
freeze, to	얼(리)다	*eol(li)da*
french fries	감자 튀김	*gamja twigim*
fresh	신선하다, 신선한	*sinseon hada, sinseon han*
Friday	금요일	*Geumyoil*
fried	튀긴	*twigin*
friend	친구	*chingu*
friendly	친절하다, 친절한	*chinjeol hada, chinjeol han*
frightened	겁먹다, 겁먹은	*geommeokda, geommeo geun*
fringe (hair)	앞머리	*ammeori*
frozen	얼다, 언	*eolda, eon*
fruit	과일	*gwa il*
fruit juice	과일 주스	*gwa il juseu*
frying pan	프라이팬	*peurai paen*
full	가득 차다/찬	*gadeuk chada, gadeuk chan*
fun, to have	재미있게 보내다	*jaemi itge bonae da*
funeral	장례식	*jangnyesik*

G

gallery	화랑	*hwarang*
game	게임	*geim*
garage (for repairs)	정비소	*jeongbiso*
garbage	쓰레기	*sseuregi*
garden, yard	정원	*jeongwon*
garlic	마늘	*maneul*
garment	옷	*ot*
gas (for heating)	가스	*gaseu*
gas station	주유소	*juyuso*
gasoline	가솔린	*gasollin*
gasoline station	주유소	*juyuso*
gate	문	*mun*
gear (car)	기어	*gieo*
gem	보석	*boseok*
gender	성별	*seongbyeol*
genuine	진짜(의)	*jinjja(ui)*
germ	세균	*segyun*
get off (transport), to	내리다	*naerida*
get on (transport), to	타다	*tada*
gift	선물	*seonmul*
ginger	생강	*saenggang*
girl	소녀	*sonyeo*
girlfriend	여자 친구	*yeoja chingu*
give, to	주다	*juda*
given name	이름	*ireum*
glad	기쁘다, 기쁜	*gippeuda, gippeun*
glass (for drinking)	컵	*keop*
glass (material)	유리	*yuri*
glasses, spectacles	안경	*angyeong*
gliding	글라이딩	*geullaiding*

glossy (photo)	광택지	*gwangtaekji*
gloves	장갑	*janggap*
glue	풀	*pul*
gnat	모기	*mogi*
go back , to	돌아가다	*dora gada*
go out, exit, to	나가다	*nagada*
go to bed, to	자다/자러가다	*jada/jareo gada*
go, to	가다	*gada*
gold	금	*geum*
golf	골프	*golpeu*
golf course	골프장	*golpeu jang*
good	좋다, 좋은	*jota, joeun*
good afternoon	안녕하세요.	*annyeong haseyo*
good evening	안녕하세요.	*annyeong haseyo*
Good luck!	행운을 빕니다!	*Haeng uneul bimnida!*
good morning	안녕하세요.	*annyeong haseyo*
good night	안녕히 주무세요.	*annyeonghi jumu seyo*
goodbye (to a person leaving)	안녕히 가세요	*annyeonghi gaseyo*
goodbye (to a person staying)	안녕히 계세요	*annyeonghi gyeseyo*
grade crossing, level crossing	철도 건널목	*cheoldo geonneolmok*
gram	그램	*geuraem*
grammar	문법	*munbeop*
grandchild	손자(M), 손녀(F)	*sonja (M), sonnyeo (F)*
granddaughter	손녀	*sonnyeo*
grandfather	할아버지, 조부	*hara beoji, jobu*
grandmother	할머니, 조모	*halmeoni, jomo*
grandparents	조부모	*jobumo*
grandson	손자	*sonja*
grape juice	포도 주스	*podo juseu*
grapes	포도	*podo*
grave	무덤	*mudeom*
graze (injury)	찰과상	*chalgwasang*
greasy	기름기 많다, 기름기 많은	*gireumkki manta, gireumkki maneun*
green	푸르다, 푸른	*pureuda, pureun*
greengrocer	야채	*yachae*
greet, to	인사하다	*insa hada*
greetings	인사말	*insa mal*
grey	회색(의)	*hoesaek(ui)*
grey-haired	백발의	*baekbarui*
grilled	굽다, 구운	*gupda, guun*
grocery	식품점	*sikpumjeom*
groceries	식품	*sikpum*
group	그룹	*geurup*
guest	손님	*sonnim*
guest house	여관	*yeogwan*
guide (book)	안내서	*annaeseo*
guide (person)	가이드	*gaideu*
guided tour	가이드가 있는 투어	*gaideuga inneun tueo*
guilty, to feel	죄책감을 느끼다	*joechaek gameul neukkida*
gym	짐	*jim*
gynaecologist	산부인과 의사	*sanbu inkkwa uisa*

H

hair	머리(카락)	*meori (karak)*
hairbrush	빗	*bit*
haircut	컷트	*keoteu*
hairdresser	미용사	*miyongsa*
hair dryer	헤어 드라이어	*he eo deura ieo*
hair spray	헤어 스프레이	*he eo seupeurei*
hair style	헤어 스타일	*he eo seuta il*
half, half full	반	*ban*
hammer	망치	*mangchi*
hand	손	*son*
hand brake	손 브레이크	*son beure ikeu*
hand luggage	휴대 수하물	*hyudae suhamul*
hand towel	손 타월	*son tawol*
handbag	핸드백	*haendeubaek*
handkerchief	손수건	*sonsugeon*
handmade	수공	*sugong*
happy	행복하다, 행복한	*haengbok hada, hangbokan*
Happy birthday!	생일 축하합니다!	*Saengil chukha hamnida!*
Happy New Year!	새해 복 많이 받으세요!	*Saehae bok mani badeu seyo!*
harbor	항구	*hanggu*
hard (difficult)	어렵다, 어려운	*eoryeopda, eoryeoun*
hard (firm)	단단하다, 단단한	*dandan hada, dandan han*
hardware	하드웨어	*hadeu we eo/hardware*
hardware store	철물점	*cheolmuljeom*
hat	모자	*moja*
have to, must	-아/어야 하다	*-a/eoya hada*
have, own, to	있다	*itda*
hay fever	꽃가루 알레르기	*kkotgaru alle reugi*
he, him	그	*geu*
head	머리	*meori*
headache	두통	*dutong*
headlights	헤드 라이트	*hedeu raiteu*
health food shop	건강 식품점	*geongang sikpumjeom*
healthy	건강하다, 건강한	*geongang hada, geongang han*
hear, to	듣다	*deutda*
hearing aid	보청기	*bocheonggi*
heart	심장, 마음	*simjang, ma eum*
heart attack	심장 마비	*simjang mabi*
heat, to	데우다	*deuda*
heater	히터	*hiteo*
heavy	무겁다, 무거운	*mugeopda, mugeoun*
heel (of foot)	발꿈치	*balkkumchi*
heel (of shoe)	굽	*gup*
Hello! (on phone)	여보세요!	*Yeoboseyo!*
Hello, Hi	안녕하세요	*Annyeong haseyo*
Help!	도와주세요!	*Dowa juseyo!*
help yourself	마음대로 드세요	*maeum daero deuseyo*
hem	단	*dan*
her	그녀의	*geu nyeoui*

herbal tea	허브 차	*heobeu cha*
herbs	허브	*heobeu*
here	여기, 이리(로)	*yeogi, iri(ro)*
hers	그녀의 것	*geunyeoui geot*
high	높다, 높은	*nopda, nopeun*
high tide	밀물	*milmul*
highway	고속도로	*gosok doro*
hiking	등산	*deungsan*
hiking boots	등산화	*deungsanhwa*
hip	힙	*hip*
hire, to	고용하다	*goyong hada*
his	그의, 그의 것	*geu ui, geu ui geot*
hitchhike	히치 하이크	*hichi haikeu*
hobby	취미	*chwimi*
holiday (public)	휴일	*hyuil*
holiday (vacation)	휴가	*hyuga*
home, house	집	*jip*
homesickness	향수병	*hyangsuppyeong*
honest	정직하다, 정직한	*jeongjik hada, jeongjikan*
honey	꿀	*kkul*
horizontal	수평이다, 수평인	*supyeongida, supyeongin*
horrible	형편없다, 형편없는	*hyeongpyeo neopda, hyeongpyeo neomneun*
horse	말	*mal*
hospital	병원	*byeongwon*
hospitality (friendly)	환대	*hwandae*
hot (spicy)	맵다, 매운	*maepda, maeun*
hot (temperature)	덥다, 더운	*deopda, deoun*
hot spring	온천	*oncheon*
hot-water bottle	보온병	*bo onbyeong*
hotel	호텔	*hotel*
hour	시간	*sigan*
house	집	*jip*
How are you?	안녕하세요?	*Annyeong haseyo?*
How far?	얼마나 멀어요?	*Eolmana meoreoyo?*
How long?	얼마나 오래요?	*Eolmana oraeyo?*
How many?	얼마나 많이요?	*Eolmana maniyo?*
How much?	얼마예요?	*Eolma yeyo?*
How old?	몇 살이에요?	*Myeot sari eyo?*
How?	어떻게요?	*Eotteoke yo?*
however	그러나	*geureona*
humid	무덥다, 무더운	*mudeopda, mudeoun*
hundred grams	백 그램	*baekgeuraem*
hungry	배고프다, 배고픈	*baego peuda, baego peun*
Hurry up!	빨리요!	*Ppalliyo!*
husband	남편	*nampyeon*
hut, shack	오두막	*odumak*

I

I, me	나, 내, 저, 제	*na, nae, jeo, je*
ice cream	아이스 크림	*aiseu keurim*
ice cubes	얼음 조각	*eoreum jogak*
ice-skating	아이스 스케이팅	*aiseu seu keiting*

English	Korean	Romanization
iced	얼다, 언	eolda, eon
idea	생각	saenggak
identification (card)	신분증	sinbunjeung
if	만일 -(으)면	manil -(eu)myeon
ignition key	차 열쇠	cha yeolsoe
ill, sick	아프다, 아픈	apeuda, apeun
illness	병	byeong
imagine, to	상상하다	sangsang hada
immediately	곧	got
import duty	관세	gwanse
important	중요하다, 중요한	jungyo hada, jungyo han
impossible	불가능하다/-한	bulganeung hada/-han
in order that, so that	-기 위해서	-gi wihaeseo
in the evening	저녁에	jeonyeoge
in the morning	아침에	achime
in, at (place)	...에(서)	...e(seo)
in-laws	처가 사람, 시댁 사람	cheoga saram, sidaek saram
included	포함되다, 포함된	poham doeda, poham doen
including	포함하다, 포함하는	poham hada, poham haneun
indicate, to	가리키다	gari kida
indicator (car)	깜박이 등	kkambagi deung
indigestion	소화불량	sohwa bullyang
inexpensive	싸다, 싼	ssada, ssan
infection	감염	gamyeom
infectious	전염되다, 전염되는	jeonyeom doeda, jeonyeom doeneun
inflammation	염증	yeomjeung
information	정보, 안내	jeongbo, annae
information office	안내소	annaeso
injection	주사	jusa
injured	다치다, 다친	dachida, dachin
innocent	결백하다, 결백한	gyeolbae kada, gyeolbae kan
insane	미치다, 미친	michida, michin
insect	벌레	beolle
insect bite	벌레 물린 상처	beolle mullin sangcheo
insect repellent	방충제	bangchungje
inside	안	anjjok
instructions	사용 설명서	sayong seolmyeongseo
insurance	보험	boheom
interested in	관심이 있다/있는	gwansimi itda/inneun
interesting	재미있다, 재미있는	jaemi itda, jaemi inneun
intermission	중간 휴식	junggan hyusik
internal	내부의	naebu ui
Internet	인터넷	Inteonet/Internet
Internet café	인터넷 카페	Inteonet kape
interpreter	통역(사)	tongyeok(sa)
intersection	교차(로)	gyocha(ro)
interview	면접	myeonjeop
introduce someone, to	소개하다	sogae hada

15

invent, to	발명하다	*balmyeong hada*
invite, to	초대하다	*chodae hada*
invoice	청구서	*cheongguseo*
iodine	요오드	*yo odeu*
iPad	아이패드	*aipae deu*
iPhone	아이폰	*ai pon*
Ireland	아일랜드	*Ail laendeu*
iron (metal)	철	*cheol*
iron (clothing), to	다리다	*darida*
ironing board	다림질판	*darim jilpan*
island	섬	*seom*
itch	가려움증	*garyeo umjeung*

J

jack (for car)	잭	*jaek*
jacket	자켓	*jaket*
jam	잼	*jaem*
January	일월	*Irwol*
Japan	일본	*Ilbon*
jaw	턱	*teok*
jeans	진	*jin*
jellyfish	해파리	*haepari*
jeweler	보석상	*boseoksang*
jewelry	보석	*boseok*
job	직업, 일	*jigeop, il*
jog, to	조깅하다	*joging hada*
joke	농담	*nongdam*
journey	여행	*yeohaeng*
juice	쥬스	*jyuseu*
July	칠월	*Chirwol*
June	육월	*Yugwol*

K

kerosene	등유	*deungyu*
key (to room)	열쇠	*yeolsoe*
kidney	신장	*sinjang*
kilogram	킬로그램	*killo geuraem*
king	왕	*wang*
kiss	키스	*kiseu*
kiss, to	키스하다	*kiseu hada*
kitchen	부엌	*bueok*
knee	무릎	*mureup*
knife	칼	*kal*
knit	니트	*niteu*
know, to	알다	*alda*
Korea, North	북한	*Bukhan*
Korea, South	남한	*Nahan*
Korean	한국 사람, 한국어	*Hanguk saram, Hangugeo*
Korean drama (K-drama)	한국 드라마	*Hanguk deurama/Hanguk drama*
Korean pop (K-pop)	한국 대중음악	*Hanguk daejung eumak*

L

English	Korean	Romanization
lace (fabric)	레이스	reiseu
laces (for shoes)	신발 끈	sinbal kkeun
ladder	사다리	sadari
lake	호수	hosu
lamb, mutton	양고기	yanggogi
lamp	등	deung
land (ground)	땅	ttang
land (plane), to	착륙하다	changnyuk hada
lane (of traffic)	차선	chaseon
language	말, 언어	mal, eoneo
large	크다, 큰	keuda, keun
last (endure)	오래가다	orae gada
last (final)	마지막이다, 마지막	maji magida, majimak
last night	지난 밤	jinan bam
later	나중에	najunge
laugh, to	웃다	utda
launderette	빨래방	ppallaebang
laundry	세탁소	setakso
law, legislation	법	beop
lawyer	변호사	byeonhosa
laxative	완화제	wanhwaje
leak, to	새다	saeda
leather	가죽	gajuk
leather goods	가죽 제품	gajuk jepum
leave, depart, to	떠나다	tteonada
left behind	남다	namda
left-hand side	왼쪽	oenjjok
leg	다리	dari
leggings	레깅즈	regingjeu
leisure	레저	rejeo
lemon, citrus	레몬	remon
lend, to	빌려주다	billyeo juda
lens (camera)	렌즈	renjeu
less (smaller amount)	더 적다/적은	deo jeokda/jeogeun
lesson	수업, 강습	su eop, gangseup
letter	편지	pyeonji
lettuce	양상치	yangsangchi
level crossing, grade crossing	철도 건널목	cheoldo geonneolmok
library	도서관	doseogwan
license (for driving)	면허증	myeonheojeung
lie (falsehood)	거짓말	geojinmal
lie down, to	눕다	nupda
lift (elevator)	엘리베이터	elli beiteo
lift (in car), to give	태워주다	taewo juda
light (lamp)	불	bul
light (not dark)	밝다/연하다, 밝은/연한	baltta/yeon hada, balgeun/yeonhan
light (not heavy)	가볍다, 가벼운	gabyeopda, gabyeoun
light bulb	전구	jeongu
lighter	라이터	raiteo
lightning	번개	beongae
like, be pleased by, to	좋아하다	joa hada

line (mark)	선	seon
line (queue)	줄	jul
linen (fiber)	린넨	rinnen
lining	안감	ankkam
liquor store	주류상	juryu sang
liquor, alcohol	술	sul
listen, to	듣다	deutda
literature	문학	munhak
litre	리터	riteo
little (amount)	적다, 적은	jeokda, jeogeun
little (small)	작다, 작은	jakda, jageun
live (be alive)	살아있는	sara inneun
live, to	살다	salda
liver	간	gan
lobster	롭스터	ropseuteo
local	지역	jiyeok
lock	자물쇠	jamulsoe
long (length)	길다, 긴	gilda, gin
look at, see, to	보다	boda
look for, to	찾다	chatda
look up (find in book), to	찾아보다	chaja boda
lose, misplace, to	잃어버리다	ireo beorida
loss (profit)	손실	sonsil
lost (can't find way)	길을 잃다/잃은	gireul ilta/ireun
lost (missing)	잃어버린	ireo beorin
lost and found office	분실물 센터	bunsilmul senteo
lotion	로션	rosyeon
loud	소리가 크다/큰	soriga keuda/keun
love	사랑	sarang
love, to	사랑하다	sarang hada
low	낮다, 낮은	natda, najeun
low tide	썰물	sseolmul
LPG	엘피지	El Pi Ji
luck	운	un
luggage	여행가방	yeohaeng gabang
luggage locker	보관함	bogwan ham
lumps (sugar)	각설탕	gakseoltang
lunch	점심 식사	jeomsim siksa
lungs	페	pye

M

madam (term of address)	부인	buin
magazine	잡지	japji
mail, post	우편물	upyeonmul
mail, to	부치다	buchida
main post office	중앙 우체국	jungang ucheguk
main road	대로	daero
make an appointment	약속하다	yaksok hada
make love	섹스하다	sekseu hada
make, create, to	만들다	mandeulda
makeshift	임시	imsi
makeup	화장	hwajang
male	남성	namseong

man	남자	*namja*
manager	관리 책임자	*gwalli chaegimja*
mango	망고	*mang go*
manicure	손톱 손질	*sontop sonjil*
many, much	많다, 많은	*manta, maneun*
map	지도	*jido*
marble	대리석	*daeriseok*
March	삼월	*Samwol*
margarine	마아가린	*ma agarin*
marina (for yachts)	정박소	*jeongbakso*
marital status	결혼 여부	*gyeolhon yeobu*
market	시장	*sijang*
married	결혼하다, 결혼한	*gyeolhon hada, gyeolhon han*
massage, to	마사지하다	*massaji hada*
mat (on floor)	깔개	*kkalgae*
mat (on table)	받침	*batchim*
match, game	시합	*sihap*
matches	성냥	*seongnyang*
matte (photo)	매트지	*maeteuji*
may	-아/어도 좋다	*-a/eodo jota*
May	오월	*Owol*
maybe	아마	*ama*
mayonnaise	마요네즈	*mayo nejeu*
mayor	시장	*sijang*
meal	식사	*siksa*
mean (word), to	의미하다	*uimi hada*
meaning	의미	*uimi*
measure out, to	재다	*jaeda*
measuring jug	계량컵	*gyeryang keop*
meat	고기	*gogi*
medicine	약	*yak*
meet, to	만나다	*mannada*
melon	참외	*chamoe*
member	회원	*hoewon*
Member of Parliament	국회의원	*Gukoe uiwon*
membership card	회원권	*hoewon kkwon*
memory card	메모리 카드	*memori kadeu, memory card*
mend, to	고치다	*gochida*
menstruation	생리	*saengni*
menu	메뉴	*menyu*
message	메시지	*messiji*
metal	금속	*geumsok*
meter (in taxi)	미터기	*miteogi*
metre	미터	*miteo*
migraine	편두통	*pyeon dutong*
mild (taste)	순하다, 순한	*sunhada, sunhan*
milk	우유	*uyu*
millimeter	밀리미터	*milli miteo*
mind, be displeased, to	신경 쓰이다	*singyeong sseu ida*
mine	내 것, 제 것	*nae geot, je geot*
mineral water	광천수	*gwangcheonsu*

minute	분	bun
mirror	거울	geoul
miss (flight, train), to	놓치다	nochida
miss (loved one), to	보고싶다, 고싶어하다	bogo sipda, bogo sipeo hada
missing	없어지다, 없어진	eopseo jida, eopseo jin
mist	안개	angae
mistake	실수	silsu
mistaken	틀리다, 틀린	teullida, teullin
misty	뿌옇다, 뿌연	ppuyeota, ppuyeon
misunderstanding	오해	ohae
mixed	섞이다, 섞인	seokkida, seokkin
mobile phone	휴대전화	hyudae jeonhwa
modern art	현대 미술	hyeondae misul
moment (instant)	순간	sungan
Monday	월요일	Woryo il
money	돈	don
monkey	원숭이	wonsungi
month	달	dal
moon	달	dal
moped	모터 자전거	moteo jajeongeo
more (comparative)	더	deo
morning	아침	achim
mosquito	모기	mogi
mosquito net	모기장	mogijang
most (superlative)	가장	gajang
motel	모텔	motel
mother	어머니	eomeoni
mother-in-law	시어머니, 장모	sieo meoni, jangmo
motorbike	오토바이	oto ba i
motorboat	모터 보트	moteo boteu
mountain	산	san
mountain hut	산장	sanjang
mouse (animal)	생쥐	saeng jwi
moustache	콧수염	kossu yeom
mouth	입	ip
movie	영화	yeonghwa
MP3 player	mp3 플레이어	Empi sseuri peullei eo/ mp3 player
MSG	조미료	Jo Mi Ryo
much, many	많다, 많은	manta, maneun
mud	진흙	jinheuk
muscle	근육	geunyuk
muscle spasms	근육 경련	geunyuk gyeongnyeon
museum	박물관	bangmulgwan
mushroom	버섯	beoseot
music	음악	eumak
must	-아/어야 하다	-a/eoya hada
my	내, 제	nae, je

N

| nail (finger, toe) | 손톱, 발톱 | sontop, baltop |
| nail (spike) | 못 | mot |

English	Korean	Romanization
nail file	손톱 줄	sontopjul
nail scissors	손톱 가위	sontop gawi
naked	벌거벗다/-벗은	beolgeo beotda/-beoseun
name	이름	ireum
nappy, diaper	기저귀	gijeogwi
nationality	국적	gukjeok
natural	자연(적인)	jayeon (jeogin)
nature	자연	jayeon
nauseous	메스껍다, 메스꺼운	meseu kkeopda, meseu kkeoun
near	가까이	gakkai
nearby	가까이에	gakka ie
necessary	필요하다, 필요한	piryo hada, piryo han
neck	목	mok
necklace	목걸이	mokgeori
necktie	넥타이	nektai
need, to	필요하다	piryo hada
needle	바늘	baneul
negative (photo)	네가티브	nega tibeu
neighbor	이웃(사람)	iut (saram)
nephew	조카	joka
never	결코...아니다/ -지 않다	gyeolko ...anida/ -ji anta
new	새롭다, 새(로운)	saeropda, sae(roun)
news	뉴스	nyuseu
news stand	신문 가판대	sinmun gapandae
newspaper	신문	sinmun
next (in line, sequence)	다음(의)	daeum(ui)
next to	...옆에	...yeope
nice	멋지다, 멋진	meotjida, meotjin
nice (pleasant)	기분 좋다, 기분 좋은	gibun jota, gibun joeun
niece	조카딸	jokattal
night	밤	bam
night duty	야간 근무	yagan geunmu
night clothes	잠옷	jamot
nightclub	나이트 클럽	naiteu keuleop
nightdress	잠옷	jamot
nipple (bottle)	젖꼭지	jeotkkokji
no (answer)	아뇨	anyo
no entry	진입금지	jinip geumji
no thank you	괜찮아요	gwaenchа nayo
no, not (with nouns)	...아니다	...anida
no, not (verbs and adjectives)	안, -지 않다	an, -ji anta
no one	아무도 ...아니다/ -지 않다	amudo ...anida/-ji anta
noise	소음	so eum
nonstop (flight)	직항	jikang
noodles	국수	guksu
normal	정상적이다/-적인	jeongsang jeogida, jeongsang jeogin
north	북쪽	bukjjok
nose	코	ko
nosebleed	코피	kopi
notebook	노트, 공책	noteu, gongchaek

notebook computer	노트북 (컴퓨터)	*noteu buk (computer)*
notepad	노트, 공책	*noteu, gongchaek*
notepaper	편지지	*pyeonjiji*
nothing	아무것도 …아니다	*amu geotdo …anida*
November	십일월	*Sibilwol*
now	지금	*jigeum*
nowhere	어디에도 … 없다	*eodi edo …eopda*
number	숫자, 번호	*sutja, beonho*
number plate	번호판	*beonopan*
nurse	간호사	*ganhosa*
nuts	밤, 호두	*bam, hodu*

O

o'clock	…시	*…si*
object, thing	물체, 사물	*mulche, samul*
occupation	직업	*jigeop*
October	시월	*Siwol*
off (gone bad)	상하다	*sanghada*
off (turned off)	꺼져 있다	*kkeojyeo itda*
offer, suggest, to	제의하다	*jeui hada*
office	사무실	*samusil*
often	자주	*jaju*
oil	기름	*gireum*
ointment	연고	*yeongo*
okay	좋다, 괜찮다	*jota, gwaenchanta*
old (of persons)	나이 많다/많은	*nai manta/maneun*
on (turned on)	켜져 있다	*kyeojyeo itda*
on board	타고 있다	*tago itda*
on foot	걸어서	*georeoseo*
on the left	왼쪽에	*oenjjoge*
on the right	오른쪽에	*oreun jjoge*
on the way	오는/가는 길에	*oneun/ganeun gire*
oncoming car	맞은편에 오는 차량	*majeun pyeone oneun charyang*
one-way ticket	편도표	*pyeondopyo*
one-way traffic	일방통행	*ilbang tonghaeng*
onion	양파	*yangpa*
open	열리다, 열린	*yeollida, yeollin*
open, to	열다	*yeolda*
operate (surgeon), to	수술하다	*susul hada*
operator (telephone)	교환	*gyohwan*
opposite (contrary)	반대(의)	*bandae (ui)*
optician	안경사, 안경점	*angyeongsa, angyeongjeom*
or	또는	*ttoneun*
orange (color)	오렌지색	*orenji saek*
orange (fruit)	오렌지	*orenji*
order (command)	주문	*jumun*
order something, to	주문하다	*jumun hada*
other	다른	*dareun*
other side	다른 쪽	*dareun jjok*
our	우리(의)	*uri(ui)*
outside	바깥(쪽)	*bakkat(jjok)*

174

outside of	...의 바깥에	...ui bakkate
over there	저기(로)	jeogi(ro)
overcome, to	이겨내다	igyeo naeda
overpass, flyover	고가도로	goga doro
overseas	해외(의)	hae oe(ui)
overtake, to	추월하다	chuwol hada
oyster	굴	gul

P

packed lunch	도시락	dosirak
page	페이지	peiji
pain	통증	tongjeung
painful	아프다, 아픈	apeuda, apeun
painkiller	진통제	jintongje
paint	페인트	peinteu
painting	그림, 칠	geurim, chil
pajamas	파자마	pajama
palace	궁	gung
pan	냄비	naembi
pane	창유리	changyuri
panties	팬티	paenti
pants	바지	baji
pantyhose	팬티 스타킹	panti seutaking
paper	종이	jongi
parasol	파라솔	parasol
parcel	소포	sopo
Pardon me?	뭐라고 하셨어요?	Mworago hasyeo sseoyo?
parents	부모	bumo
park (car), to	주차하다	jucha hada
park, gardens	공원	gongwon
parking garage	차고	chago
parking space	주차장	juchajang
parliament	국회	gukho e
part (of machine)	부속	busok
partner (in business)	동업자	dongeopja
partner (spouse)	배우자	bae uja
party (event)	파티	pati
passenger	승객	seunggaek
passport	여권	yeokkwon
passport photo	여권 사진	yeokkwon sajin
password	비밀번호, 암호	bimil beonho/amho
patient (calm)	인내심 있다/-있는	innae simitda/-inneun
patient (doctor's)	환자	hwanja
pay (bill), to	지불하다	jibul hada
peach	복숭아	boksunga
peanut	땅콩	ttangkong
pearl	진주	jinju
peas	완두콩	wandukong
pedal	페달	pedal
pedestrian crossing	건널목	geonneolmok
pedicure	발톱 손질	baltop sonjil
pen	펜	pen
penalty	벌금	beolgeum

pencil	연필	yeonpil
penis	(남성) 성기	(namseong) seonggi
penknife	주머니 칼	jumeoni kal
people	사람들	saramdeul
pepper, black	후추	huchu
pepper, chili	고추	gochu
performance	공연	gongyeon
perfume	향수	hyangsu
perhaps, maybe	아마	ama
period (menstrual)	생리	saengri
permit, allow, to	허락하다	heorak hada
person	사람	saram
personal	개인적이다, 개인적인	gaein jeogida, gaein jeogin
pet animal	애완동물	aewan dongmul
petrol	휘발유	hwiballyu
petrol station	주유소	juyuso
pharmacy, drugstore	약국	yak guk
phone	전화	jeonhwa
phone, to	전화하다	jeonhwa hada
phone booth	전화 박스	jeonhwa bakseu
phone card	전화 카드	jeonhwa kadeu
phone directory	전화 번호부	jeonhwa beonhobu
phone number	전화 번호	jeonhwa beonho
photo (digital)	(디지털) 사진	(dijiteol) sajin
photocopier	복사기	boksagi
photocopy	복사	boksa
photocopy, to	복사하다	boksa hada
photograph	사진	sajin
photograph, to	사진 찍다	sajin jjikda
phrasebook	숙어집	sugeojip
pick up (someone), to	태워주다	taewo juda
picnic	야유회	yayu hoe
pillow	베개	begae
pillowcase	베갯잇	begaesh it
pills, tablets	알약	allyak
pin	핀	pin
pineapple	파인애플	pa inae peul
pipe (plumbing)	파이프	pa ipeu
pipe (smoking)	파이프	pa ipeu
pipe tobacco	파이프 담배	pa ipeu dambae
place of interest	관광 명소	gwangwang myeongso
plain (not flavored)	담백하다/-한	dambaek hada, dambae kan
plain (simple)	단순하다, 단순한	dansun hada, dansun han
plan	계획	gyehoek
plane	비행기	bihaenggi
plant	식물	singmul
plastic	플라스틱	peulla seutik
plastic bag	비닐 봉지	binil bongji
plate	접시	jeopsi
platform	플랫폼	peullaet pom
play (drama)	연극	yeongeuk

English-Korean Dictionary

play (fun), to	놀다	nolda
play golf	골프 치다	golpeu chida
play sports	운동 경기하다	undong gyeonggi hada
play tennis	테니스 치다	teniseu chida
playground	운동장	undongjang
playing cards	카아드 놀이	kadeu nori
pleasant	기분 좋다/좋은	gibun jota/joeun
please (request)	좀 -어/아 주세요	jom -eo/a juseyo
pleasure	기쁨	gippeum
plug (electric)	플러그	peulleo geu
plum	자두	jadu
pocket	호주머니	ho jumeoni
pocketknife	주머니 칼	jumeoni kal
point out, to	지적하다	jijeok hada
poison	독(약)	dok(yak)
poisonous	독이 있다/있는	dogi itda/inneun
police	경찰	gyeongchal
police officer	경찰관	gyeongchal gwan
police station	경찰서	gyeongchalseo
pond	연못	yeon mot
pony	조랑말	jorangmal
pop music	대중음악	daejung eumak
population	인구	ingu
pork	돼지고기	dwaeji gogi
port	항구	hanggu
porter (concierge)	수위	suwi
porter (for bags)	포터	poteo
possible	가능하다, 가능한	ganeung hada, ganeung han
post office	우체국	ucheguk
post, mail, to	부치다	buchida
postage	우편 요금	upyeon yogeum
postage stamp	우표	upyo
postbox	우체통	uchetong
postcard	엽서	yeopseo
post code	우편 번호	upyeon beonho
postpone, to	연기하다	yeongi hada
potato	감자	gamja
potato chips	감자 튀김	gamja twigim
powdered milk	분유	bunyu
power outlet	콘센트	konsenteu
prawn	새우	sae u
precious metal	귀금속	gwigeumsok
precious stone	보석	boseok
prefer, to	선호하다	seonho hada
preference	선호	seonho
pregnant	임신하다, 임신한	imsin hada, imsin han
prescription	처방(전)	cheo bang (jeon)
present (gift)	선물	seonmul
present (here)	출석하다, 출석한	chulseok hada, chulseok kan
press, journalism	언론	eollon
pressure	압력	amnyeok

177

price	가격	gagyeok
price list	가격표	gagyeok pyo
print (photo)	인화	inhwa
print, to	인화하다	inhwa hada
probably	아마	ama
problem	문제	munje
profession	직업	jigeop
profit	이익	i ik
program, schedule	프로그램	peuro geuraem
pronounce, to	발음하다	bareum hada
propane	프로판 가스	peuropan gaseu
pudding	푸딩	puding
pull a muscle	근육 이완	geunyuk iwan
pull, to	당기다	danggida
pulse	맥박	maekbak
pure	순수하다, 순수한	sunsu hada, sunsu han
purple	자주색	jajusaek
purse (for money)	지갑	jigap
push, to	밀다	milda
puzzled	어리둥절하다/	eori dungjeol hada
pyjamas	파자마	pajama

Q

quarter	4 분의 1	sa bunui il
quarter of an hour	십오분	sipobun
queen	여왕	yeowang
question	질문, 문제	jilmun, munje
quick	빠르다, 빠른	ppareuda, ppareun
quiet	조용하다, 조용한	joyong hada, joyonghan

R

radio	라디오	radio
railroad, railway	철도	cheoltto
rain	비	bi
rain, to	비가 오다	biga oda
raincoat	비옷	bi ot
rape	강간	ganggan
rash	발진	baljin
rat	쥐	jwi
rate of exchange (for foreign currency)	환율	hwannyul
rate, tariff	요금	yogeum
raw, uncooked	날 (것의)	nal (geosui)
razor blade	면도날	myeondonal
read, to	읽다	ilktta
really (in fact)	실제로	siljero
Really?	정말요?	Jeongmaryo?
reason	이유	iyu
receipt	영수증	yeongsujeung
receive, to	받다	batda
reception desk	안내	annae
recipe	조리법	jori beop
recommend, to	추천하다	chucheon hada

rectangle	직사각형	*jiksa gakhyeong*
red	빨갛다, 빨간	*ppalgata, ppalgan*
red wine	적포도주	*jeokpo doju*
reduction	축소	*chukso*
refrigerator	냉장고	*naengjanggo*
refund	환불	*hwanbul*
region	지역, 지방	*jiyeok, jibang*
registered	등록되다, 등록된	*deungnok doeda, deungnok doen*
relatives, family	친척	*chincheok*
reliable	믿을 만하다, 믿을 만한	*mideulman hada, mideulman han*
religion	종교	*jonggyo*
remains (historical)	유물	*yumul*
rent out, to	세주다	*sejuda*
rent, to	임대하다	*imdae hada*
repair, to	고치다	*gochida*
repeat, to	반복하다	*banbok hada*
report (police)	보고서	*bogoseo*
reservation	예약	*yeyak*
reserve (ask for in advance), to	예약하다	*yeyak hada*
responsible, to be	책임 있다/있는	*chaegim itda/inneun*
rest, relax, to	쉬다	*swida*
restaurant	식당	*sikdang*
restroom	화장실	*hwajangsil*
result	결과	*gyeolgwa*
retired	퇴직하다, 퇴직한	*toejik hada, toeji kan*
return ticket	왕복표	*wangbokpyo*
reverse (car), to	뒤로 가다	*dwiro gada*
rheumatism	류머티즘	*ryumeo tijeum*
ribbon	리본	*ribon*
rice (cooked)	밥	*bap*
rice (grain)	쌀	*ssal*
rice (plant)	벼	*byeo*
ride, to	타다	*tada*
ridiculous	어리석다, 어리석은	*eori seokda, eori seogeun*
riding (horseback)	말타기	*maltagi*
right of way	지금 당장	*jigeum dangjang*
right, correct	옳다, 옳은	*olta, oreun*
right-hand side	오른쪽	*oreun jjok*
rinse	헹굼	*henggum*
ripe, to	익다, 익은	*ikda, igeun*
risk	위험	*wiheom*
river	강	*gang*
road	도로	*doro*
roadway	차도	*chado*
roasted, grilled, toasted	구운	*gu un*
rock (stone)	바위	*bawi*
roll (bread)	롤빵	*rolppang*
roof	지붕	*jibung*
room	방, 룸	*bang, rum*
room number	룸 넘버	*rum neombeo*
room service	룸 서비스	*rum seobiseu*

rope	밧줄	*batjul*
route	루트	*ruteu*
rowing boat	나룻배	*narutbae*
rubber	고무	*gomu*
rude	무례하다, 무례한	*murye hada, murye han*
ruins	유적	*yujeok*
run, to	달리다	*dallida*
running shoes	조깅화	*joginghwa*

S

sad	슬프다, 슬픈	*seulpeuda, seulpeun*
safe	안전하다, 안전한	*anjeon hada, anjeon han*
safe (for cash)	금고	*geumgo*
safety pin	안전핀	*anjeon pin*
sail, to	항해하다	*hanghae hada*
sailing boat	요트	*yoteu*
salad	샐러드	*saelleodeu*
sale (reduced prices)	세일	*seil*
sales clerk	점원	*jeomwon*
salt	소금	*sogeum*
salty	짜다, 짠	*jjada, jjan*
same	같다, 같은	*gatda, gateun*
sandals	샌달	*saendal*
sandy beach	백사장	*baeksajang*
sanitary towel, sanitary napkin	생리대	*saengnidae*
satisfied	만족하다	*manjok hada*
Saturday	토요일	*Toyo il*
sauce	소스, 양념	*soseu, yangnyeom*
saucepan	냄비	*naembi*
sauna	사우나	*sa una*
save, keep, to	보관하다	*bogwan hada*
say, to	말하다	*mal hada*
scald (injury)	물화상	*mul hwasang*
scales	저울	*jeo ul*
scan, to	스캔하다	*seukaen hada/scan hada*
scarf	스카프	*seukapeu*
scenic walk	전망이 좋은 산책로	*jeonmangi joeun sanchaeng no*
school	학교	*hakgyo*
scissors	가위	*gawi*
Scotland	스코틀랜드	*Seukoteul laendeu*
screw	나사	*nasa*
screwdriver	드라이버	*deu raibeo*
scuba diving	스쿠버 다이빙	*seukubeo daibing*
sculpture	조각	*jogak*
sea	바다	*bada*
seafood	해물	*haemul*
seasick	배멀미	*baemeolmi*
seat	자리	*jari*
second (in line)	두 번째	*du beonjjae*
second (instant), in a	금방	*geumbang*
second-hand	중고	*junggo*
sedative	진정제	*jinjeongje*

English	Korean	Romanization
see, to	보다	*boda*
send, to	보내다	*bonaeda*
sentence	문장	*munjang*
separate	각각(의)	*gakgak(ui)*
September	구월	*Guwol*
serious	심각하다, 심각한	*simgak hada, simgak han*
service	서비스	*seobiseu*
service station	주유소	*juyuso*
serviette, table napkin	냅킨	*naepkin*
sesame oil	참기름	*chamgi reum*
sesame seeds	참깨	*chamkkae*
set	세트	*seteu*
sew, to	바느질하다	*baneu jilhada*
shade	그늘	*geuneul*
shame, disgrace	수치	*suchi*
shampoo	샴푸	*syampu*
shark	상어	*sangeo*
shave, to	면도하다	*myeondo hada*
shaver	면도기	*myeondo gi*
shaving cream	면도 크림	*myeondo keurim*
she	그 여자	*geu yeoja*
sheet (for bed)	시트	*siteu*
shirt	셔츠	*syeocheu*
shoe polish	구두약	*guduyak*
shoes	신발	*sinbal*
shop assistant	점원	*jeomwon*
shop window	쇼 윈도우	*syo windou*
shop, go shopping, to	쇼핑하다	*syoping hada*
shop, store	가게	*gage*
shopping center	쇼핑 센터	*syoping senteo*
short (not tall)	작다, 작은	*jakda, jageun*
short circuit	합선	*hapseon*
shorts (short trousers)	반바지	*banbaji*
shorts (underpants)	팬티	*paenti*
shoulder	어깨	*eokkae*
show (live performance)	쇼	*syo*
show, to	보여주다	*boyeo juda*
shower, to take a	샤워하다	*syawo hada*
shrimp, prawn	새우	*saeu*
shutter (camera, on window)	셔터	*syeoteo*
sick, ill	아프다, 아픈	*apeuda, apeun*
sieve	체	*che*
sightseeing	시내 관광	*sinae gwangwang*
sign (road)	도로 표지	*doro pyoji*
sign, symbol	표시	*pyosi*
sign, to	서명하다	*seomyeong hada*
signature	서명,사인	*seomyeong, ssa in*
silent	고요하다, 고요한	*goyo hada, goyohan*
silk	실크	*silkeu*
silver	은	*eun*
similar	비슷하다, 비슷한	*biseut hada, biseu tan*
simple (easy)	쉽다, 쉬운	*swip da, swi un*
simple (uncomplicated)	간단하다/-한	*gandan hada, gandan han*

English	Korean	Romanization
sing, to	노래하다	norae hada
single (only one)	단 하나(의)	dan hana(ui)
single (unmarried)	독신(의)	doksin (ui)
single ticket	편도표	pyeondopyo
sir (term of address)	…님	…nim
sister	자매	jamae
sit down, to	앉다	anda
size	사이즈	saijeu
skiing	스키	seuki
skin	피부	pibu
skirt	치마	chima
Skype address	스카이프 주소	seukai peu juso/Skype juso
sleep, to	자다	jada
sleeping car	침대칸	chimdaekan
sleeping pills	수면제	sumyeonje
sleeve	소매	somae
slip (petticoat, underskirt)	슬립	seullip
slippers	슬리퍼	seullipeo
slow	느리다, 느린	neurida, neurin
slow train	완행 열차	wanhaeng yeolcha
slowly	천천히	cheoncheonhi
small	작다, 작은	jakda, jageun
small change	잔돈	jandon
smart phone	스마트폰	seuma teupon/smart phone
smell, bad odor	냄새	naemsae
smoke	연기	yeongi
smoke (tobacco), to	담배 피다	dambae pida
smoke detector	연기 경보기	yeongi gyeongbogi
snake	뱀	baem
sneeze, to	재채기하다	jaechaegi hada
snore, to	코 골다	ko golda
snorkel	스노클링	seuno keulling
snow	눈	nun
snow, to	눈이 오다	nuni oda
soap	비누	binu
soap powder	세제	seje
soccer	축구	chukgu
soccer match	축구 경기	chukgu gyeonggi
socket (electric)	소케트	soketeu
social media (Social Networking Service or SNS)	소셜 미디어/SNS	sosyeol midi eo/social media/SNS
socks	양말	yangmal
soft drink	음료수	eumnyosu
software	소프트웨어	sopeuteu we eo/software
sold out	매진	maejin
sole (of shoe)	밑창	mitchang
somebody, someone	어떤 사람	eotteon saram
something	어떤 것	eotteon geot
sometimes	가끔	gakkeum
somewhere	어딘가	eodinga
son	아들	adeul
soon	곧	got

sore throat	인후통	*inhutong*
sore, painful	아프다, 아픈	*apeuda, apeun*
Sorry!	미안합니다!	*Mian hamnida!*
soup (clear)	국	*guk*
soup (spicy stew)	찌개	*jjigae*
sour	시다, 신	*sida, sin*
south	남쪽	*namjjok*
souvenir	기념품	*ginyeom pum*
soy sauce	간장	*ganjang*
spanner, wrench	스패너	*seuppae neo*
spare	스페어	*seuppe eo*
spare parts	부품	*bupum*
spare tyre/wheel	스페어 타이어	*seuppeo taieo*
speak, to	말하다	*mal hada*
specialist (doctor)	전문의	*jeon munui*
speciality (cooking)	특선 요리	*teukseon yori*
speed	속도	*sokdo*
speed limit	제한 속도	*jehan sokdo*
spell, to	철자하다	*cheoljja hada*
spices	양념, 향료	*yang nyeom, hyang nyo*
spicy	맵다, 매운	*maepda, mae un*
splinter	파편	*papyeon*
spoon	숟가락	*sukkarak*
sports	스포츠	*seupocheu*
sports center	스포츠 센터	*seupocheu senteo*
spot (place)	지점	*jijeom*
spot (stain)	점	*jeom*
spouse	배우자	*bae uja*
sprain	삠	*ppim*
spray	스프레이	*seupeurei*
spring (device)	용수철	*yongsucheol*
spring (season)	봄	*bom*
square (plaza)	광장	*gwangjang*
square (shape)	정사각형	*jeongsa gakhyeong*
square meter	제곱 미터	*jegop miteo*
squash (game)	스쿼시	*seukwosi*
squid	오징어	*ojing eo*
stadium	스타디움	*seuta dium*
staff	직원	*jigwon*
stain	얼룩	*eolluk*
stain remover	얼룩 제거제	*eolluk jegeoje*
stairs	계단	*gyedan*
stamp (postage)	우표	*upyo*
stand up, to	일어서다	*ireo seoda*
star	별	*byeol*
start, beginning	시작	*sijak*
start, to	시작하다	*sijak hada*
station	역	*yeok*
stationery	문구	*mungu*
statue	동상	*dong sang*
stay overnight, to	묵다	*mukda*
stay, remain, to	머무르다	*meomu reuda*
steal, to	훔치다	*humchida*

steamed	찌다, 찐	jjida, jjin
steel	강철	gangcheol
stepfather	계부	gyebu
stepmother	계모	gyemo
steps, stairs	계단	gyedan
sterilise, to	소독하다	sodok hada
sticking plaster	반창고	banchanggo
sticky tape	테프	tepeu
stitch (in wound), to	봉합하다	bonghap hada
stomach (abdomen)	배	bae
stomach (organ)	위	wi
stomach ache	복통	boktong
stomach cramps	위 경련	wi gyeongnyeon
stone	돌	dol
stools (feces)	대변	daebyeon
stop (bus)	정류장	jeongnyujang
stop, cease	그만두다	geuman duda
stop, halt to	멈추다	meomchuda
stopover	도중 하차	dojung hacha
store, shop	가게	gage
storey (of a building)	...층 짜리	...cheung jjari
storm (weather)	폭풍	pokpung
straight	똑바르다, 똑바른	ttokba reuda, ttokba reun
straight ahead	똑바로	ttokbaro
straw (drinking)	스트로	seuteuro
street	거리	geori
street vendor	자동 판매기	jadong panmaegi
strike (work stoppage)	파업	pa eop
string	끈	kkeun
strong	힘세다, 힘센	himseda, himsen
student	학생	haksaeng
study (learn), to	공부하다	gongbu hada
stuffed animal	동물 인형	dongmul inhyeong
subtitles	자막	jamak
succeed, to	성공하다	seonggong hada
sugar	설탕	seoltang
suit, business	정장	jeongjang
suitcase	여행가방	yeohaeng gabang
summer	여름	yeoreum
sun	태양	taeyang
sunbathe	일광욕	ilgwangyok
Sunday	일요일	Iryo il
sunglasses	선글라스	seongeullas
sunlight	햇빛	haetbit
sunny	화창하다/-한	hwachang hada/-han
sunrise	일출	ilchul
sunscreen	썬탠 크림	seontaen keurim
sunset	일몰	ilmol
sunshade	차일	cha il
sunstroke	일사병	ilsa byeong
suntan lotion	썬탠 로션	seontaen rosyeon
suntan oil	썬탠 오일	seontaen oil
supermarket	수퍼마켓	supeo maket

surcharge	추가 요금	*chuga yogeum*
surf	파도	*pado*
surface mail	선편	*seonpyeon*
surfboard	서핑 보드	*seoping bodeu*
surname	성	*seong*
surprised	놀란	*nollan*
swallow, to	삼키다	*samkida*
swamp	습지	*seupji*
sweat	땀	*ttam*
sweat, to	땀 흘리다	*ttam heullida*
sweater	스웨터	*seuweteo*
sweet	달다, 단	*dalda, dan*
sweetcorn	사탕 옥수수	*satang oksusu*
sweets, candy	사탕	*satang*
swim, to	수영하다	*suyeong hada*
swimming costume, swimsuit	수영복	*suyeong bok*
swimming pool	수영장	*suyeong jang*
swindle	사기	*sagi*
switch	스위치	*seuwichi*
syrup	시럽	*sireop*

T

table	테이블	*teibeul*
table tennis	탁구	*takgu*
tablecloth	테이블 보	*teibeul bo*
table mat	접시 받침	*jeopsi batchim*
tablespoon	테이블 스푼	*teibeul seupun*
tablets	알약	*allyak*
tableware	식탁용구	*sikta kyonggu*
take (medicine), to	(약을) 먹다	*(yageul) meokda*
take (photograph), to	(사진을) 찍다	*(Sajineul) jjikda*
take (time), to	(시간이) 걸리다	*(sigani) geollida*
take off (clothes), to	벗다	*beotda*
talk, to	말하다	*malhada*
tall	키 크다/큰	*ki keuda/keun*
tampon	탬폰	*taempon*
tap	수도	*sudo*
tap water	수돗물	*sudon mul*
tape measure	줄자	*julja*
taste	맛	*mat*
taste, to	맛보다	*mat boda*
tasty, delicious	맛있다, 맛있는	*masitda, masinneun*
tax	세금	*segeum*
tax-free shop	면세점	*myeon sejeom*
taxi	택시	*taeksi*
taxi stand	택시 정류장	*taeksi jeongnyujang*
tea	차	*cha*
tea (green)	녹차	*nokcha*
tea cup	찻잔	*chatjan*
teapot	차 주전자	*cha jujeonja*
teaspoon	티 스푼	*ti seupun*
teat (bottle)	젖병 꼭지	*jeotbyeong kkokji*
teeth	이	*i*

telephoto lens	망원 렌즈	*mangwon lenjeu*
television	텔레비전	*telle bijeon*
tell, to	말하다	*malhada*
temperature (body)	체온	*cheon*
temperature (heat)	온도	*ondo*
temple	절	*jeol*
temporary filling	임시 때움	*imsi ttae um*
tender (sore)	무르다 무른	*mureuda, mureun*
tennis	테니스	*teniseu*
tent	텐트	*tenteu*
terminus	종점	*jongjeom*
terrace	테라스	*teraseu*
terribly	몹시	*mopsi*
test	시험	*siheom*
text message	문자 (메시지)	*munja (mesiji)/munja (message)*
Thank you!, Thanks!	감사합니다!	*Gamsa hamnida!*
thaw, to	녹이다	*nogida*
theater (drama)	극장	*geukjang*
theft	도난	*donan*
there	저기에, 거기에	*jeogi e, geogi e*
thermometer (body)	체온계	*cheongye*
thermometer (weather)	온도계	*ondogye*
they	그들	*geudeul*
thick (of liquids)	진하다, 진한	*jinhada, jinhan*
thick (of things)	두껍다, 두꺼운	*dukkeopda, dukkeoun*
thief	도둑	*doduk*
thigh	허벅지	*heobeokji*
thin (not fat)	마른	*mareun*
thin (not thick)	묽은	*mulgeun*
thing	물건	*mulgeon*
think, have an opinion, to	생각하다	*saenggak hada*
think, ponder, to	숙고하다	*sukgo hada*
third	세 번째	*se beonjjae*
third, one third	삼분의 일	*sambune il*
thirsty	목마르다, 목마른	*mongma reuda, mongma reun*
this afternoon	오늘 오후	*oneul ohu*
this evening	오늘 저녁	*oneul jeonyeok*
this morning	오늘 아침	*oneul achim*
thread	실	*sil*
throat	목(구멍)	*mok (gumeong)*
throat lozenges	기침 사탕	*gichim satang*
thunderstorm	천둥 폭풍우	*cheondung pokpungu*
Thursday	목요일	*Mogyo il*
ticket	표	*pyo*
ticket office	매표소	*maepyoso*
tidy	단정하다, 단정한	*danjeong hada, danjeong han*
tie (necktie)	넥타이	*nektai*
tie, to	매다	*maeda*
tights, pantyhose	타이즈	*taijeu*
time (occasion)	시간	*sigan*

English	Korean	Romanization
times (multiplying)	...배	...bae
timetable	시간표	siganpyo
tin (can)	깡통	kkangtong
tin opener	깡통 따개	kkangtong ttagae
tip (gratuity)	팁	tip
tissues	티슈	tisyu
tobacco	담배	dambae
today	오늘	oneul
toddler	유아	yua
toe	발가락	balkkarak
together	함께	hamkke
toilet	화장실	hwajangsil
toilet paper	화장지	hwajangji
toilet seat	변기	byeongi
toiletries	세면 도구	semyeon dogu
tomato	토마토	tomato
tomorrow	내일	naeil
tongue	혀	hyeo
tonight	오늘밤	oneul ppam
tool, utensil, instrument	도구	dogu
tooth	이	i
toothache	치통	chitong
toothbrush	칫솔	chissol
toothpaste	치약	chiyak
toothpick	이 쑤시개	i ssusigae
top	꼭대기	kkokdaegi
top up, to	채우다	chae uda
torch, flashlight	손전등	sonjeondeung
total	합계	hapgye
tough	거칠다, 거친	geochilda, geochin
tour	투어	tueo
tour guide	투어 가이드	tueo gaideu
tourist	관광객	gwangwanggaek
tourist class	투어 클라스	tueo keullaseu
tourist information office	관광 안내소	gwangwang annaeso
tow, to	끌다	kkeulda
tow cable	케이블	keibeul
towel	수건	sugeon
tower	탑	tap
town	마을, 시	maeul, si
town hall	구청	gucheong
toy	장난감	jangnankkam
traffic	교통	gyotong
traffic light	신호등	sinhodeung
train	기차	gicha
train station	역	yeok
train ticket	기차표	gichapyo
train timetable	기차 시간표	gicha siganpyo
translate, to	번역하다	beonyeok hada
travel agent	여행사	yeohaengsa
travel, to	여행하다	yeohaeng hada
traveler	여행자	yeohaengja
traveler's cheque	여행자 수표	yeohaengja supyo

English-Korean Dictionary

15

tree	나무	*namu*
triangle	삼각형	*samgakhyeong*
trim (haircut), to	(머리를) 다듬다	*(meorireul) dadeumda*
trip, journey	여행	*yeohaeng*
trouble	문제	*munje*
trousers	바지	*baji*
truck	트럭	*teureok*
trust, to	믿다	*mitda*
trustworthy	믿을만한	*mideul manhan*
try on (clothes), to	입어보다	*ibeo boda*
try on (footwear), to	신어 보다	*sineo boda*
try on (headgear), to	써보다	*sseo boda*
tube (of paste)	튜브	*tyubeu*
Tuesday	화요일	*Hwayo il*
tuna	참치	*chamchi*
tunnel	터널	*teoneol*
turn off, to	끄다	*kkeuda*
turn on, to	켜다	*kyeoda*
turn over, to	뒤집다	*dwijipda*
TV	티비	*Ti Bi*
TV guide	티비 방송안내	*Ti Bi bangsong annae*
tweet	트위터하다	*teuwiteo hada/Twitter hada*
Twitter	트위터	*Teuwiteo/Twitter*
tweezers	족집게	*jokjipge*
twin bed	트윈 베드	*teuwin bedeu*
typhoon	태풍	*taepung*
tyre	타이어	*ta ieo*
tyre pressure	타이어 압력	*ta ieo amnyeok*

U

ugly	못생기다, 못생긴	*motsaeng gida, motsaeng gin*
ulcer	궤양	*gweyang*
umbrella	우산	*usan*
under	...아래	*...arae*
underpants	팬티	*paenti*
underpass	지하도	*jihado*
understand, to	이해하다	*ihae hada*
underwear	속옷	*sogot*
undressed, to get	옷 벗다	*ot beotda*
unemployed	실직한	*siljikan*
uneven	고르지 않은	*goreuji aneun*
university	대학	*daehak*
unleaded	무연	*muyeon*
until	...까지, -(으)ㄹ 까지	*...kkaji, -(eu)l ttaekkaji*
up, upward	...위에, ...위로	*...wi e, ...wiro*
upright	똑바른, 똑바로	*ttokba reun, ttokbaro*
urgent	긴급한	*gingeupan*
urgently	긴급하게	*gingeu page*
urine	소변	*sobyeon*
USB flash drive	USB (메모리 카드)	*Yu e Seu Bi (memori kadeu)*

| use, to | 사용하다 | *sayong hada* |
| usually | 보통 | *botong* |

V

vacate, to	비우다	*bi uda*
vacation	방학	*banghak*
vaccination	예방 접종	*yebang jeopjong*
vagina	(여성) 성기	*(yeoseong) seonggi*
valid	유효하다, 유효한	*yuhyo hada, yuhyo han*
valley	계곡	*gyegok*
valuable	귀중하다, 귀중한	*gwijung hada, gwijung han*
valuables	귀중품	*gwijung pum*
van	봉고차	*bonggocha*
vase	꽃병	*kkotbyeong*
vegetables	야채	*yachae*
vegetarian	채식주의자	*chaesik ju uija*
vein	정맥	*jeongmaek*
velvet	벨벳	*belbet*
vending machine	자동 판매기	*jadong panmaegi*
venomous	독이 있다, 독이 있는	*dogi itda, dogi inneun*
venereal disease	성병	*seongbyeong*
vertical	수직이다, 수직(인)	*suji gida, sujig(in)*
very	아주	*aju*
vest, undershirt	조끼	*jokki*
via	...을/를 거쳐서	*...eul/reul geochyeoseo*
video camera	비디오 카메라	*bidio kamera*
video recorder	비디오 (레코드)	*bidio (rekodeu)*
view, look at, to	보다	*boda*
view, panorama	경치	*gyeongchi*
village	마을	*maeul*
vinegar	식초	*sikcho*
visa	비자	*bija*
visit	방문	*bangmun*
visit, to pay a	방문하다	*bangmun hada*
visiting time	방문 시간	*bangmun sigan*
visual (virtual) conference	화상 회의	*hwasang hoe ui*
vitamin tablets	비타민(제)	*bitamin(je)*
vitamins	비타민	*bitamin*
volcano	화산	*hwasan*
volleyball	배구	*baegu*
vomit, to	토하다	*tohada*

W

wait for, to	기다리다	*gida rida*
waiter, waitress	종업원	*jongeo bwon*
waiting room	대기실	*daegisil*
wake someone up, to	깨우다	*kkae uda*
wake up, to	깨어나다	*kkae eonada*
walk (noun)	걷기	*geotgi*
walk, to	걷다	*geotda*
walking stick	지팡이	*jipangi*
wall	벽	*byeok*
wallet	지갑	*jigap*

want, to	...을/를 원하다, -고 싶다	...eul/reul wonhada, -go sipda
wardrobe	옷장	otjang
warn, to	경고하다	gyeonggo hada
warning	경고	gyeonggo
wash, to	씻다	ssitda
washing	세탁	setak
washing machine	세탁기	setakgi
wasp	벌	beol
watch (wristwatch)	(손목)시계	(sonmok) sigye
watch, look, see, to	보다	boda
water	물	mul
water-skiing	수상 스키	susang seuki
waterfall	폭포	pokpo
watermelon	수박	subak
waterproof	방수	bangsu
way (direction)	쪽	jjok
way (method)	방법	bangbeop
way in	입구	ipgu
way out	출구	chulgu
we, us	우리	uri
weak	약하다, 약한	yak hada, yakhan
wear, to	입다	ipda
weather	날씨	nalssi
weather forecast	일기예보	ilgi yebo
wedding	결혼식	gyeolhonsik
Wednesday	수요일	Suyo il
week	주	ju
weekday	주중	jujung
weekend	주말	jumal
weigh, to	...의 무게를 달다	...ui muge reul dalda
weigh out, to	달아내다	dara naeda
Welcome!	어서 오세요!	Eoseo oseyo!
well (for water)	우물	umul
well (good)	잘	jal
west	서쪽	seojjok
Westerner	서양 사람	Seoyang saram
wet	젖다, 젖은	jeotda, jeojeun
What?	뭐라고요?	Mwora goyo?
wheel	바퀴	bakwi
wheelchair	휠체어	hwilche eo
When?	언제요?	Eonjeyo?
whenever	-(으)ㄹ 때마다	-(eu)l ttae mada
Where to?	어디로 가세요?	Eodi ro gaseyo?
Where?	어디요?	Eodi yo?
Which?	어느 거요?	Eoneu geoyo?
white	하얗다, 하얀	hayata, hayan
white wine	백포도주	baekpo doju
Who?	누구요?	Nuguyo?
Why?	왜요?	Waeyo?
widow	과부	gwabu
widower	홀아비	horabi
wife	아내	anae

wind, breeze	바람	*baram*
window (for paying, buying tickets)	창구	*changgu*
window (in house)	창문	*changmun*
windscreen wiper	와이퍼	*waipeo*
windscreen, windshield	(자동차) 앞유리	*(jadong ha) amnyuri*
wine	와인	*wain*
winter	겨울	*gyeoul*
wire	철사	*cheolssa*
wireless connection	무선 인터넷	*museon inteonet*
wish, to	바라다	*barada*
witness	목격자	*mokgyeokja*
woman	여자	*yeoja*
wonderful	멋지다, 멋진	*meotjida, meotjin*
wood	나무	*namu*
wool	울, 양모	*ul, yangmo*
word	단어	*daneo*
work, occupation	일, 직업	*il, jigeop*
work, to	일하다	*ilhada*
working day	근무일	*geunmu il*
worn out (clothes)	닳아버리다/-버린	*dara beorida, dara beorin*
worn out, tired	피곤하다, 피곤한	*pigon hada, pigon han*
worry, to	걱정하다	*geokjeong hada*
wound	상처	*sangcheo*
wrap, to	싸다	*ssada*
wrench, spanner	스패너	*seupaeneo*
wrist	손목	*sonmok*
write down	적다	*jeokda*
write, to	쓰다	*sseuda*
writing pad	공책	*gongchaek*
writing paper	편지지	*pyeonjiji*
wrong (mistaken)	틀리다, 틀린	*teul lida, teullin*

Y

yawn	하품	*hapum*
year	년	*nyeon*
years old	...살, ...세	*...sal, ...se*
yellow	노랗다, 노란	*norata, noran*
yes	네, 예	*ne, ye*
yes please	네, 그렇게 해 주세요	*ne, geureoke hae juseyo*
yesterday	어제	*eoje*
you (audience)	여러분	*yeoreobun*
you (familiar)	너, 너희(들)	*neo, neohui(deul)*
you (female)	아가씨, 아주머니	*agassi, a jumeoni*
you (male)	아저씨, 선생님	*ajeossi, seon saengnim*
You're welcome (to "Thanks!")	괜찮아요!	*Gwaencha nayo!*
youth hostel	유스 호스텔	*yuseu hoseutel*

Z

zip (fastener)	지퍼	*jipeo*
zoo	동물원	*dongmulwon*
zucchini	애호박	*aehobak*

"Books to Span the East and West"

Tuttle Publishing was founded in 1832 in the small New England town of Rutland, Vermont [USA]. Our core values remain as strong today as they were then—to publish best-in-class books which bring people together one page at a time. In 1948, we established a publishing office in Japan—and Tuttle is now a leader in publishing English-language books about the arts, languages and cultures of Asia. The world has become a much smaller place today and Asia's economic and cultural influence has grown. Yet the need for meaningful dialogue and information about this diverse region has never been greater. Over the past seven decades, Tuttle has published thousands of books on subjects ranging from martial arts and paper crafts to language learning and literature—and our talented authors, illustrators, designers and photographers have won many prestigious awards. We welcome you to explore the wealth of information available on Asia at **www.tuttlepublishing.com**.

Published by Tuttle Publishing, an imprint of Periplus Editions (HK) Ltd.

www.tuttlepublishing.com

Copyright © 2017 Periplus Editions (HK) Ltd

All rights reserved. No part of this publication may be reproduced or utilized in any form or by any means, electronic or mechanical, including photocopying, recording, or by any information storage and retrieval system, without prior written permission from the publisher.

Library of Congress Control Number: 2016955384

ISBN: 978-0-8048-4680-6

Second edition
25 24 23 22 21
10 9 8 7 6 5
2111TP

Printed in Singapore

TUTTLE PUBLISHING® is a registered trademark of Tuttle Publishing, a division of Periplus Editions (HK) Ltd.

Distributed by

North America, Latin America & Europe
Tuttle Publishing
364 Innovation Drive
North Clarendon, VT 05759-9436 U.S.A.
Tel: 1 (802) 773-8930; Fax: 1 (802) 773-6993
info@tuttlepublishing.com
www.tuttlepublishing.com

Japan
Tuttle Publishing
Yaekari Building 3rd Floor 5-4-12 Osaki
Shinagawa-ku, Tokyo 141 0032
Tel: (81) 3 5437-0171; Fax: (81) 3 5437-0755
sales@tuttle.co.jp; www.tuttle.co.jp

Asia Pacific
Berkeley Books Pte. Ltd.
3 Kallang Sector #04-01, Singapore 349278
Tel: (65) 6741-2178; Fax: (65) 6741-2179
inquiries@periplus.com.sg
www.tuttlepublishing.com

Indonesia
PT Java Books Indonesia
Jl. Rawa Gelam IV No. 9
Kawasan Industri Pulogadung
Jakarta 13930, Indonesia
Tel: 62 (21) 4682 1088; Fax: 62 (21) 461 0206
crm@periplus.co.id; www.periplus.com